Josephine Jamieson was born in Ayr on February 9th 1956 to James and Freda Anderson. She lived in Aberdeen later in life for 31 years. She was a mother of four, until her eldest child Dean was brutally taken away from her through murder. This is her story.

Dedications

Grampian Police
Faye Tough (Liaison Officer)
Adrian Brewster (Liaison Officer)
Alan Smith (Detective Superintendent)
Adrian Cottam (Prosecutor for the Queen)
My Family

Josephine Kennedy Smart
Jamieson

LAST TOUCH

AUSTIN MACAULEY
PUBLISHERS LTD.

A CIP catalogue record for this title is available from the British Library.

ISBN 9781786293565 (Paperback)
ISBN 9781786293572 (Hardback)
ISBN 9781786293589 (E-Book)
www.austinmacauley.com

First Published (2017)
Austin Macauley Publishers Ltd.
25 Canada Square
Canary Wharf
London
E14 5LQ

Acknowledgments

To my dearly beloved son Dean who gave me the courage to write this book and to his children Lauren, Liam, Keelan and Tyler who are a credit to him. To my other three children Paul, Gareth and Kerrie and their partners who have brought me such joy and have given me such wonderful grandchildren. Jordan, Connor, Olivia, Joshua, Cooper, Georgia and Rebecca who have brought me such happiness. To Carol my daughter-in-law, Dean's wife, who singlehandedly ensured that the boys have turned into happy well adjusted nice young men to be proud of and Mellissa, Lauren's mother, a granddaughter who has grown into a lovely caring young woman. My brothers Tony, Kevin and John and extended family and last but not least my husband Gordon who keeps me balanced. The list goes on. I am blessed to have the best family and friends in the world. Special thanks goes to Andrew Jobling who encouraged me to write this book and have faith in me when I had none.

Contents

Chapter 1

Surviving the Death of a Beloved Child

You can survive, you have to for the sake of your family. Your life never to be the same again. You are thrust into a black tunnel, an abyss that is never ending. There is no light at the end. Minutes turn into hours, hours turn into days, days turn into weeks, and weeks turn into years. They merge together like a big dark cloud hanging over you. There is a void right where your heart is that reaches down to your womb where you once carried your child. No pain is greater than losing a child, never mind the needless slaying of them. But you can get through it. You are thrown into a violent raging sea in which you are tossed and battered as you try to reach the surface. You think if I can just reach the top and gasp for air you will survive. The pain was physical, there was no relief. The world that you once knew would be no more.

I ate the tasteless food that was set before me. Sleep was no relief as it brought with it disturbing nightmares. I walked and talked and went about my business, but that person was not me, it was someone else. Yes, you contemplate suicide. I did not want to live with such ongoing pain, the anguish was tearing me apart. I wanted the pain to stop, only it wouldn't go away. I wanted to be with Dean, to hear him laugh, to hear him cry. I wanted him to call me in the middle of the night to pick him up so that I could get mad, like I always did. *Why didn't he call me that night?* I wonder. The realisation that you will never see or hear your child again is too much to bear. I ached to hold him one last time, to tell him that I would make it better, like I did when he was a child. When I would rock him to sleep and tell him no one would ever hurt him. How wrong was I?

In the aftermath of a violent death your life is in chaos, questions are asked constantly over and over again by the police and the media. You have to inform your relatives and friends. This is the most difficult conversation you will ever have. My two youngest children knew that their brother was dead before me. I had to inform my son who was living in England at the time, or rather my youngest son informed his brother, it was devastating for him. My husband was working in New Zealand at the time and can be a nightmare to contact, but for some strange reason when I phoned him he answered straight away. I cannot remember speaking to my husband, but I must have as he arrived home on the next available flight. My mother and brothers were the next people that I called, but by that time I was on auto pilot.

Yet, you can survive. Friends and neighbours would visit, food and flowers were dropped off. One particular friend, a medium, visited to offer her condolences. She said that Dean had told her that I was contemplating suicide. I looked at her through glazed and red eyes and could only nod. I felt embarrassed. "Jo," she said, "if you do, then you won't be with your dad or your son, so there would be no purpose. What about your other children, don't they matter?"

I was shocked and stunned by what she had said. It was the shake that I needed. I was so wrapped up in my own pain that I never gave my family or other children a thought. My pain was so great that I had totally withdrawn from everyone. Yes, I was answering the police and the media's questions, making meals, doing the washing and all the normal things that you do. Only, I was not normal and in my place was a stranger, a bitter, angry person who was full of rage. It was a long time before that stranger left and I could once again live and laugh or even make plans.

From the very first time that I heard about Dean's horrific death the scene was set and I became a player in an unexpected scenario, for which I had no script. I didn't know fully what was going on. I was in shock, in disbelief, and horrified. I knew I was answering questions and I knew that my family was beside me, but I couldn't breathe. I was slowly falling into the regions of hell, a bottomless pit from which I struggled to get out of. But you do survive. Sometimes when you are experiencing trauma you don't realise that you need help, or how to ask for it. In my case, I wouldn't let anyone help me. I was wrong and it was selfish of me. I was not the only person hurting, but I was acting as if I was. Family and friends were too afraid to say anything for fear of me spiralling way out of control, if only they had. I was paralysed with fear, not knowing what to do. I believed that it was my duty to carry the burden. He was my child and I couldn't protect him as I promised, so I died a little every day.

I know differently now, I should have shared the grief, it was not only mine to own. Dean had a wife, children, brothers, and a sister. He also had grandmothers and uncles and many more family and friends who were all deeply affected by his horrific murder. They had lost someone dear and important too. I never acknowledged their grief, I couldn't see it; I was too far gone and I had totally disengaged from the world and my only way of survival was to be in control.

My oldest grandson was drowning and he had started hitting his head on the floor for no reason; something that was totally out of character for him. I knew he needed help, but we, his family, were in no position emotionally to provide him with that help and support.

I contacted the Children's Counselling Service, only to be told that there was a six month waiting list. I was so enraged. I worked as a social worker and was aware that the four people who had murdered my son had access to social workers, counsellors and psychologists.

The victim's family had access to a 6 month waiting list. Where was the fairness in that? I refused to take no for an answer. I had lost my son and I was not going to let his son suffer any more than he already had. Liam, age eight, was in pain and struggling. He couldn't understand why four men had brutally murdered his dad. The children were provided with a counsellor and she was to be Liam's salvation. It allowed him to grieve for his dad without him fearing that he was burdening his family. He told me that he was afraid to speak about his dad with us in case it upset us and he didn't want to see his mum cry anymore.

It became my mission to make sure that my son's children received all the support that they needed so I contacted Winston's Wish, the charity for bereaved children, including those affected by death through murder and manslaughter. It is located in a place in England called the Forest of Dean, how apt. It offers families practical advice in the immediate days and weeks when violence has been the cause of death. It aims to give parents and professionals the confidence to involve and support children. It includes practical activities for families as they begin to make sense of what has happened and start to look at ways in which the family can learn to cope and move forward. The two older boys and their mother Carol stayed at the Forest of Dean for a long weekend. It allowed the children to share their experience with other children and families and gave Carol a long earned rest where she received valuable information on how to support the children. The youngest boy was too young to attend. Dean also has a daughter who lived with her mother. She was also offered to attend, but her mother felt that she was coping well.

I once tried counselling, but that wasn't for me. What did she know? Had she lost a child to murder? She didn't know how I was feeling. I was not in a good place, only I didn't see it. I even ran away for a couple of nights as I had no place to hide, no place that I could just think. People were everywhere, they even followed me to the toilet. I knew I was on suicide watch but I didn't care. I couldn't bear the look of pity, or the comfort people offered me. I almost wanted to feel the pain – yes, pain was good. My poor broken son had suffered real pain, mine was superficial.

I went to a retreat, set in a beautiful location in the Black Isle in Inverness right in the middle of the highlands, secluded from the world. There was a lovely cottage with a view of the sea at the front and a rugged forest at the back of the house. It was so peaceful. It was run by a woman who was a lay preacher and her friend. She was a kind soul. I immediately felt at home in the house. The preacher picked me up from the train station and advised me that I was the only client that would be staying in the house that night until the next day when they would be expecting a few more people. She informed me that she had a little cottage close by or asked if I would rather she stayed in the main cottage. I was afraid to ask her to stay in case she thought I was odd, so I told her that I would be okay on my own. We drove the rest of the journey in silence. I was grateful for the peace and quiet.

I had taken many books with me, most of which were spiritual, one in particular was *Talking to Heaven* by James Van Praagh. It was about a medium's message of life after death. I was desperate to know that my son was safe and with my father who had passed many years before. Books were to be my salvation. It was what got me through each day. I think I cried buckets. This was something I was unable to do at home as there were always people around. Their beady eyes focussed on the paracetamol bottle in case I felt like ending it. 'It' meaning life. I holed myself up in my room only venturing out for meals, or the occasional walk in the forest, or to let the sea breeze wash over my face. There is something relaxing and invigorating when the breeze catches your face and the taste of the salty sea is in your mouth.

The first night in my room was very surreal. I had not been alone for quite some time. I cried myself to sleep, it was like a dam bursting, once started I couldn't stop. I think I may have dozed as a lady came into my room and patted me on the shoulder. I was afraid to look up. I asked the lay preacher in the morning if she had come into my room during the night, she said that she hadn't and that the house was not haunted. It was to happen one more night. It brought me comfort.

A while later I visited a medium who made reference to the nightly visit and said that Dean had sent an angel to comfort me. Visiting mediums also helped me survive. A telephone call I would say. I knew I could become addicted. I was desperate. As time went by I needed them less, although, I still access them for my

17

telephone call. People find many ways that help them get through the early days, such as counselling, family, or like me, books and mediums. I know that you cannot get through it on your own. On reflection, the lesson that I have learned is not to push people away. I believe that if I had sought help earlier life would have been different. I would have been able to face my demons and to grieve for Dean and who he was. Instead, the dark passenger called rage came to live with me for a while stopping the grieving process. If there is one thing that I have learned that is to talk to someone, it doesn't necessarily mean a counsellor. It could be a friend, a minister, or even a stranger. Don't shut out the people that you love.

Chapter 2

I am Dean

I was but a mere child at school when I first encountered Dean's dad. My friend and I were dancing at Prestwick's first disco, the Bow and Arrow club. We were both underage, but my friend's mother cleaned for the owners. I was dancing to Elton John's *Crocodile Rock* when this handsome, arrogant boy asked me for a dance. I was smitten straight away. We arranged to meet again. I was fourteen years old, nearly fifteen, and lied about my age. I fell head over heels, blinded by love. He was a bit of a bad boy I later found out, that added to the excitement. The law and he didn't often see eye to eye. We had a very tumultuous relationship filled with fun and laughter, but mostly tears.

So you can imagine the horror that my father felt when I informed him that his precious little girl at age 18 years was getting married. His eyes welled with tears and he begged me to reconsider. I was torn, but I was in love and wanted the happy ever after that he and my mother had. Was that so wrong? I wanted the dream, the house, and the children. I was too young to understand. My mother was in Australia nursing her dying mother when I called to tell her the good news. Mother was struck dumb and speechless for once in her life and advised me that we would speak when she returned home, her undertone threatening, meaning *no, you're not.* I can be a very determined person. "I'm not changing my mind," I told her.

It was with a heavy heart that my father walked me down the aisle, begging me to change my mind. So, on a beautiful summer day in July, the sun shining, the sky blue, and the flowers blowing gently in the wind at St Quivox church Whitletts Ayrshire, we became man and wife until death do us part. It was a typical 1970's wedding, much to the horror of my parents who, despite their misgivings, begrudgingly provided the trappings for our church wedding.

We rented a flat in Prestwick and for a while I was happy to play the doting wife, although married life was not what I had expected, that is until I fell with child. I was ecstatic, over the moon. It was one year and one month after I said 'I do' on the 6th August 1975 at 15.10 when Dean came screaming into the world, not sure if he wanted to be here. He had left his cosy shelter that had been his home for the past nine months and more. He had to be helped into this world, so arrived kicking and screaming and no doubt left the same way I'm sure. At six pounds and nine ounces a beautiful bundle of joy.

I could not believe that this perfect little boy was my baby. I gazed at his little elfin face and a gush of overwhelming love washed over me. I was nineteen years old and a mother. It was almost surreal. I would place him on my bed and draw the curtains and stare at him for what seemed an eternity. This came to an abrupt and sudden end when the nurse caught me in the act as you are not allowed to put babies on the bed. That day I gazed lovingly at my firstborn and made a promise to him that I would be the best mother I could and protect him from all harm. Only I didn't protect him, did I?

The cracks of my marriage were beginning to appear, the fighting and arguing escalating until it came to a point where I feared for our lives. Worried that my son would get hurt and that I couldn't protect him, I left the marriage for good. I appeared at my parent's home, tail between my legs, waiting for those immortal words, *I told you so.* Thankfully it never came, we were welcomed back into the fold where I once more felt safe, vowing to always listen to my parent's advice, they knew better.

So here I was: a single parent, the fairy-tale ended. It was me and him, time to start a new life upwards and onwards. It was scary, the future, what would it bring? I was only nineteen years old with the responsibility of this precious little life. I now know that we were too young, two children playing happy families. Dean's father was never part of Dean's childhood, but he knew who he was and chose not to be involved with him, although he had met him on a few occasions. Dean would *say I have a real dad and a biological dad,* that being my husband Gordon whose name he was eventually to bear.

Dean was a happy but hyper child, always full of beans. He could never sit still for a minute. *Sit at peace,* you would hear me say, but he never could. I would often sit and marvel about how blessed I was for my first born child had brought me such happiness and joy. I would sometimes be gripped with fear in case I had damaged him in some way having married his dad, could he have his traits, would he be like him? Thank God he never was. I won't say he was an angel either, he was human, and he had his faults like we all have.

Two years later I met my second husband. I thought I won't go for the good looking arrogant type. This time I won't let my heart rule my head. He was a computer operator, sensible with a good job and serious. Two years later we married having already produced a beautiful son, Paul. We relocated to Aberdeen to begin our married life together. This too was short-lived. He turned out to be a womaniser. Heavily pregnant with my third child on Father's Day he chose to exit from our lives, two days before our beautiful son Gareth was born. It always did amaze me that he chose to do the same thing that his father did to him. He would get upset when he relayed how his own father had been detained for embezzlement and how it had affected his life. The soulless bastard forgot to tell us he wasn't coming back, leaving me to believe that he had been involved in a serious accident. I was frantically trying to make sense of what was going on, lying to my parents in case they found out what a failure I had become again.

Having contacted Missing Persons he was located by the local police in England. Missing adult persons who are otherwise well and healthy can 'elect not to be found' and the duty police are duty bound to honour that. I received a call three weeks later from the husband of the woman he had left with. She left behind a seven year old son. Well, I guess I started thinking that perhaps me and relationships don't work and I would be better off with myself and my children. I was the only person who my children could rely on as their absent fathers found it difficult to provide for either of their needs, financially or emotionally.

This took its toll on Dean, who had not only lost the only father that he knew, he was starting school and had a new brother. Behaviour tantrums appeared where none were present before, he started wetting the bed and getting upset over the smallest things. We managed to work through things, but I think it scarred him for life especially in his own personal relationships as he grew older.

It was one of those horrible, dreary days as I walked Dean to school, pushing the pram with the new baby and a toddler on top. I decided I needed to provide for my children to give them a good life with financial security. I set myself some goals. It is amazing what goes through your head as you trundle through your mundane life. One of them goals was to pass my driving test. I was twenty-four years old and very isolated living in the suburb of Westhill, Aberdeenshire, eight miles from the city with three young children and I needed wheels.

I also wanted to become a black belt in Aikido, and the third was to return to school and get some qualifications. I succeeded in two out of three of those goals, not bad, never having the time to attend Aikido much due to my responsibilities. Having not much money to spare I sat with the kids at school, no coffee mornings for me. So, when I was getting Dean ready for school, Paul ready for nursery and the baby dropped off at the crèche, schoolbag in hand, I rushed into the classroom. The teacher would raise his eyebrows and say, "Late again Josephine," how I hated my Sunday name. The kids at school would giggle when I got told off for being late, as I uttered under my breath the words, "Sorry sir."

A few months later, my knight in shining armour walked into our lives. He was tall, blond, and a good looking, easy-natured man who I met at a local club. We had a dance or two and then he gave me and friends a lift home.

Before he had a chance to ask me for a date my sassy friend said, "If you would like to meet her again she will be at the Broadstraik Inn tomorrow night."

Never expecting him to turn up, low and behold, my knight in shining armour appeared at the Inn. "Would you like a drink?" he said.

"Sure," I replied.

My friend Maria said, "Tell him Jo."

Gordon asked, "Tell me what?"

"I'm married," I said, "but separated."

"Okay," said Gordon, "would you like another drink?"

"Sure," we replied.

Maria said, "Tell him."

Gordon, "Tell me what?"

"I've got a child."

Gordon, "Oh really, would you girls like another drink."

"Sure," we replied.

Marie, "Just tell him Jo."

Gordon, "No more drink for you girls."

"I've actually got three kids."

Gordon asked to be excused as he needed to go to the toilet. I thought, *oh well, last time I'll see him again.*

So it was a great surprise when I saw him grinning in the doorway. "Anything else to tell me before I sit down?" he asked.

"No, that's it," I replied.

A story the children never cease to tire of. So Gordon Alexander Jamieson entered our lives and became the father my children never had. He was never a step father, or their biological father either, but their real father as they would testify to. For that I am filled with pride and admiration for Gordon. Two years later I finally had that girl, a beautiful, blue eyed blond. We named her Kerrie-Louise. My family was complete. I had it all.

Gordon worked offshore and was often away for months at a time, so technically I was still a single mother. I continued with my education and graduated at university in Radiography and after a short career I returned to university to study Psychology, and then a post graduate in Social Work at Master's level, whilst working at various jobs, such as children's homes, to fund my studies. I often wonder how I survived in those days, with little sleep I'm sure. I later became a social worker and continue to work in that field now. We were one big happy family - where did it all go wrong?

As Dean grew up he led a normal happy life, playing football, writing songs, and so forth. He decided hairdressing would be his career of choice and then he found girls. He was always a bit of a ladies' man, a bit of "Jack the lad", always the clown, a charmer to say the least, and true to style he followed his mother's footsteps and fell in love at the age of eighteen. By nineteen he was the father of a beautiful baby girl. A year later his bubble burst, the relationship had gone sour, never to return. Dean was devastated and drink became his best friend. There was no consoling him and we had to ride the storm. No fairy-tale ending for him but he still had his daughter and she was forever in his life, *his one bright light*, he used to say. Dean had many jobs and one would lead him to the woman who was to eventually become his wife.

Married at twenty-one, to his wife four years his senior, Dean tried to fit everything in. From a young age he felt the need to tell me that he had to live as he was going to die by the age of thirty. "Don't be stupid," I'd say. On his thirtieth birthday he rang me up to say that he might after all have got it wrong, I was exasperated with him. It was eight months after his thirtieth birthday that he was so callously slain, by a group of thugs who acted like a pack of animals. Maybe it was that Dean had wanted a family of his own that he married young, always the dreamer, a romantic at heart as he wed his strawberry blond girl with the wayward hair and blue eyes.

Carol was his boss when they met and shortly after, his lover. A shy, quiet girl who was soon to be a part of our mad but close family. Dean would often say, "Our family is a bit like the Osbournes, but without the swearing," as when they all got together it was chaos, laughter and fighting, one big happy family. I think Carol thought this family was totally nuts. I remember the day that he got wed, it was a beautiful sunny day and the smell of cherry blossom was wafting through the house from the old tree in the garden as the door was always left open. "Shut that door," I often screamed and the usual reply in unison by all four kids would be, "what door?"

As usual the house was filled with noise, people rushing around, screaming, "It's my turn for the bathroom next," or, "Who's moved my shoes?" I took a minute to reflect and sighed as I thought, *where has the time gone*? It was only yesterday that he was born and

27

now my baby was getting married with another child on the way, as Carol was heavily pregnant. They didn't want a big wedding, no fuss, just immediate family. It was the first time that I had seen him so nervous, practicing his speech with his siblings teasing him. He looked so young as his father fixed his tie. I heard him say his vows with a heavy heart as I would no longer be his number one lady in his life, he had a wife now. Tears were slowly trickling down my face. I hurriedly wiped them away as I didn't wish anyone to see them. The house was going to be so quiet when he was gone, the first to fly the nest.

Almost immediately he became the house-husband and took over the job caring for the children. It made perfect sense as his wife had the greater earning capacity borne out of an already established career. Dean had a multitude of jobs in the past and would soon tire of them thinking that something better would come along. He would often say, "I just haven't found my niche yet." For a while it worked, Dean being the stay-at-home parent, but it was too quiet for Dean and loneliness would set in with nobody to have a conversation with except a baby. He was used to a house filled with noise, laughter, and fighting. He started drinking to ease the boredom, loneliness, frustration, and feeling of uselessness. He always was a bit of drinker and when things got stressful he would tend to binge drink, but this was different as he was a father with responsibilities. Carol, his wife, eventually gave her job up.

It was as a father that Dean excelled and he couldn't give that up, he didn't want to be like his biological father and not be a part of their lives. He wanted to be there when they woke up and when they went to bed. His marriage was failing and they had become more like companions, the passion gone. The strain of being married young and having three young children with Carol and another child with a previous girlfriend had taken its toll on their lives, but he couldn't leave. He was like a fish out of water, fighting for survival. Every now and again Dean would disappear for a couple of days and binge drink and that would scare me as he always saw the good in everyone, he was vulnerable and he was an annoying but happy drunk.

Dean hid behind alcohol, he had lost his confidence and he drank so he didn't have to think, he was unhappy and he didn't know how to change it, so he took time out as he would say. He thought of himself as a singer and would burst into song when drunk, the trouble with his singing was at most times it was unwelcome by others. It nearly landed him a couple of black eyes as he didn't realise that they were not the friends that he thought they were. So if he was not singing he would be showing whoever would, or would not, look at the pictures of his children. His last act before his slaughter was spent showing the four animals who murdered him in cold blood the pictures of his children as he pled to be returned home to them. His final thoughts as a living breathing human were for his children and family. It is a matter of record with the Scots High Court. Something I want his children to know is how much he loved them.

Dean was never afraid to cry, to sympathise or empathise and openly demonstrate his love for others, especially his children. They were the lights of his life the one true and good thing he had ever done he would say. He would often phone at inappropriate times to tell me something cute they had done, or to get one of them to sing me a song or recite a nursery rhyme they had learned. His children would make him laugh and it was at these moments when you would see Dean truly happy. He was a big kid himself and would love to play with them. He once told me that his greatest fear would be if he never saw them. I think that was the reason him and Carol never separated. They were in a relationship of convenience. Dean would say that he would always love Carol as she gave him the greatest gift of all, three wonderful sons. Although their marriage was over, love and respect remained.

Dean wasn't an alcoholic but your typical binge drinker. Whether it was a release that he needed I don't know, but what I do know is that often or not he would not be alone. His wife knew and chose to ignore it for whatever reason she had. I would rage at Dean and he'd get mad and would say, "I have needs, end of story." Right or wrong, we all accepted it. Dean's greatest strength was his faith and trust in human nature and his greatest weakness was alcohol: the two of them together led to his downfall and murder.

Dean was a brother to Paul, Gareth and Kerrie and they were like normal siblings who fought and laughed, one minute hating each other and the next supporting one and other. Family always came first. It disturbed his siblings when he would disappear as they knew he was vulnerable. The boys would also get angry and, yes, embarrassed when he got drunk as he became the clown, the singer, or whatever took his fancy. They were young and impressionable. However, when Dean was not drinking they would look up to him as he was their older brother and they would tease each other.

Dean supported Celtic and Paul, Gareth and Gordon supported Rangers, and on match days the house would be filled with noise and all sorts of profanities, all in good nature. Kerrie and Dean were very alike and because she was the only girl he was protective of her. They also used to tease and play games on each other; one of these was a ritual that they used to play every time Dean would visit. As he left the house he would run up to Kerrie and say, "Last touch," and this would last for a few minutes. I would laugh and say, "Don't you guys ever grow up," and they would just laugh. It is a memory that I cannot block out and I would do anything to hear them say it one last time, I was forbidden to touch Dean as I would contaminate the investigation. My son who lay there lying on a cold and soulless slab in the police mortuary became an investigation. I ached to hold him to take away the fear that was in his eyes.

Yes, you survive the death of a child, but it takes time. With help and support you can live a happy and fulfilled life, but there is a process and as a parent you have to walk that journey.

Chapter 3

The Knock on the Door

It was on the 4th April, very late in the evening. I had been visiting a friend and was a little tired as I had just recently returned from Australia after visiting family. We had a few drinks and watched the George Best Story. I remembered sitting, wondering if Dean would be watching the documentary as he loved documentaries and George Best, according to Dean, was the best footballer ever to play for Manchester United and Northern Ireland. He was also his biggest critic as he believed that George Best had been given a second chance at life and had destroyed it having fallen off the wagon again. He was infuriated that he had abused someone else's organ that had been given to him in order that he could live. He had violated the precious gift of life that was presented to him.

I often wondered where Dean found his profound sense of morality and justice. It bothered him that people did the wrong thing and I used to smile as Dean could not see that sometimes he also done the wrong thing. George Best was charismatic and a notorious womaniser, a young man who had left his beloved Ireland behind. It was a case of too much too soon. Best could not cope with fame and fortune and drink became his ally. He was always on the front page of the newspapers for his latest conquest and drunken rampage and the back page for his sporting prowess. Dean had similarities to George Best: both played football, although Dean played for fun, Best was a professional. Both enjoyed a drink - maybe a bit too much - both were good looking and both were fun-loving and cheeky chaps.

I really cannot remember the time as I was just dozing off in bed as I was still suffering from jet lag. I was snuggling down thinking it wasn't so long ago when I was wrestling with the heat wearing next to nothing, now wrapped up like a sausage roll. I recalled the phone call that I had recently received whilst I was on holiday in Australia and Dean had called to ask if he could return home as things were not working out with Carol and it was affecting the children. He said that he couldn't go on. I informed him that there would be rules and that of course he could come home, but that I would not put up with him disappearing and going on drunken binges.

"That's fine," said Dean.

I half-expected him to be there when I returned from holiday, but he wasn't. I guessed they must have worked things out. The noise woke me up and I heard my son

Gareth's voice. Fear gripped me to the core. I knew it had to be serious for Gareth to come to the house. I was afraid to move. I lay there silently trying not to breathe hoping I was hearing things. Never in my wildest imagination would I be prepared for what I was about to be told.

My friend appeared in the doorway saying that Gareth and another man were there and wanted to speak with me.

"What is it?" I asked, but there was no reply.

My heart was thudding wildly and I felt it was about to pop out my chest as fear gripped my very soul. I looked first at Gareth and saw raw naked fear in his eyes. What could be so bad that could render my son in the grips of hell? My eyes darted from one to the other. *What is it?* I screamed silently as I couldn't speak, no words would come out. I was paralysed with fear. The man that accompanied Gareth was small in stature and was wearing jeans. I was a bit confused when I saw them and wondered why Gareth had brought this man to my friend's house. He looked at me with pity in his eyes fearing the words he had to utter.

"We have found a body covered in tattoos and believe it to be your son, Dean."

"No!" I screamed, "you're wrong!" as I darted from one to another. "Dean is not covered in tattoos so you are wrong." Gareth looked on helplessly and my friend who was sitting on the floor could not look up. "It's not true, they're lying!" I screamed, blind panic taking hold.

They asked me to accompany them to my house which was two minutes down the road. I could not breathe, something was stuck in my throat that was preventing me from speaking. I was having a bad dream only I couldn't waken. This was not happening to me. It was not happening to the family. You hear about these things in the newspaper, only it happens to other people.

As I arrived at my house another detective was present as well as the neighbours. I remember thinking *why are they here?* I didn't want them there to listen to the horror story that was about to unfold. I wanted to tell them to go away but I couldn't. Elaine ran to hug me.

"Don't," I cried, "just don't touch."

She stopped in her tracks, "I'm so, so, sorry," she said.

I couldn't take it in. Kerrie, a shrunken figure, who looked like the wind had been knocked out of her was sitting next to Detective Chapman, a tall sturdy man. All eyes focused on me wondering what I was going to do next. I collapsed onto the nearest chair as my legs no longer could hold me. Questions were being asked and I believe I answered them only I cannot remember. Time stood still, the room was going round and round and inside I was spinning out of control.

Eventually, the detectives left and Gareth, Kerrie and myself were left alone with our thoughts. We were shell-shocked, stunned and we could not make sense of what had just unfolded. No one touched or spoke, each living their own nightmare, scared to utter a word in case it was true. We were scared, we would crumble. It was a dark, cold morning and the snow covered the ground, the road was treacherous, when we left the house to make the terrible journey to Dean's house and find out how Carol was coping with the terrible news. I knew she would have been home alone and knowing her would not have contacted her family for support.

We drove the twenty minutes to Kemnay in silence, still afraid to speak with tears streaming down our faces. It felt like we were on an eternal roller coaster and it just wouldn't stop. As we approached the house it appeared different, the lights were glaring and it seemed unwelcoming. I braced myself as we entered the house afraid what we might see. The Liaison Officers - Faye Tough and Adrian Brewster - were with Carol my daughter-in-law, at the home she shared with Dean and their children, breaking the awful news to her that her husband of nearly ten years was dead. The man that she had dropped off some hours before was never coming home She was in shock as she tried to answer their questions. Adrian was sitting on Dean's chair and I remember thinking *he needs to get off his chair*, bizarre thoughts going through my head.

It struck me then how compassionate both Adrian and Faye were, both trying to be as sensitive as possible but knowing that they had to try and get as much information as possible. Time was of the essence. Research shows that the more information you have early on in an investigation, the better the results. I looked at Carol who was staring back at me with the eyes of a frightened rabbit.

I literally fell onto the settee as we listened to more of the details of Dean's last movements unravel. They had had an argument and after, Carol dropped Dean off at the Criterion Bar in Aberdeen across from the bus station. The children were in the car and the last words that Carol had uttered were, "Don't come back, we're finished." They were words that came back to haunt her. I tried to reassure Carol that Dean was coming home and that he had heard the same words a number of times and never took any heed of them. The children were sleeping and the house was like a morgue, fitting for the conversations that were taking place. It was normally filled with noise and the shrieking sound of the children's laughter. We left the house as the sun rose; Gareth and I, emotional wrecks having been spun out to dry. I left Kerrie behind to support Carol and help her explain to the boys that their dad was never coming home again. At that point we never knew he had been murdered.

The journey home was harrowing, each locked in our own world, in uncharted territory. The world we once knew gone forever and we were suspended in time. I didn't know what to do, should I call people and let them know, but that would mean it had happened and Dean would not be coming home. Fatigue took over and the need to be alone consumed me. I climbed the stairs with a heavy heart, as I made the journey to my bedroom. I threw myself upon my bed and sobbed until I could not sob anymore. Drained and exhausted I eventually fell asleep. There is no warning, no time to say goodbye, no time to put things into order, no time to tell your loved one that you love them, instead you are thrust into a world of terror and grief.

I woke up that day to the sound of the telephone ringing. As I rushed to answer it, it hit me like a stone and the memory came rushing back that Dean was gone. I missed the call. I started phoning my family before they found out by other means, that being the press. It was the hardest conversation that I ever had to make. I cannot remember much in the next few days that followed, only that the house was full of people. Gordon was home from New Zealand and my family had travelled from Ayr to be by my side. The media of course was ever-present. Each day brought more information and each day brought more grief and pain as the whole sordid story began to emerge that Dean had been murdered. Oh God, it couldn't get any worse, my poor son, who could have done this heinous act, was it a song gone wrong? Dean had no enemies that we knew of. Adrian and Faye, the Liaison Officers, were now a constant presence in our home, piecing together every last minute of Dean's life.

Detective Alan Smith who was the chief investigator had requested that he would like to have a meeting with Carol and myself. Gordon had not yet arrived home. We held a family meeting beforehand and we decided that we all had questions to ask and that the meeting should take place with all of us present. It was with anticipation and trepidation that that we all traipsed up at Bucksburn police station - my brother Kevin, my remaining children Paul, Gareth, Kerrie, Dean's wife Carol and me. We were taken into a room that I was very familiar with. It was the room that we used to interview children and families who are involved in a sensitive crime and it was much more comfortable than a police station. The familiar blue suite and cheery room started to close in on me. Seeing it in a different light brought goose bumps to my body. Fear for what we were about to be told had gripped our very soul.

Sitting in the room that I knew so well, now appeared cold and unwelcoming as we waited for Detective Alan Smith to arrive. Adrian had spoken to me and advised us that he had spoken with Alan and he would only speak with me and Carol. I informed Adrian that we had a family meeting and that Alan would have to speak with us all. Adrian stated that Alan had agreed to speak with us under duress and that he was not happy and would be having words with him later. He later told us that Alan had been glad that Adrian had put him in a predicament that had forced him to speak with the family as we were co-operative and willing to engage and work with the police in trying to bring whoever had murdered Dean to justice, thus making their job easier.

I have since heard through the police that sometimes families proportion blame to the police that they claim that they are not doing enough to find the killers and it makes relationships difficult and harder to work with. As a family we just wanted the perpetrator to be caught and brought to justice. Relationships with the police were always good and they explained every step of the way what was happening and we were always kept in the loop. For that as a family, we are eternally grateful for the support they gave us.

We were then taken into a conference room where Alan asked us more questions on Dean's habits and advised us that they now believed that Dean had been murdered. It was a harrowing experience as I listened to him explain in graphic detail the horrific injuries that had been inflicted upon my poor battered son. Alan said that they had then stripped him naked to freeze and bleed to death in the snow. The weather conditions were well below freezing in a lonely secluded location next to Craibstone golf course on Elrick Hill, where they had left him to die.

I was angry and full of guilt that I was not there to stop what happened to Dean. I would have done anything, instead I could do nothing. It happened and I should have been there to protect him like I promised when he was a baby. I was in a state, there was no one there, Dean was all alone and all I could think of was the fear he must have felt at what was happening as they tortured and humiliated him during their frenzied, pack mentality, animalistic, attack. With every word that Alan uttered a knife was twisted in my heart. I wanted to run, to put my hands across my ears. *No more* I silently said, but I knew I had to endure it as Dean endured his savage beating.

We went home exhausted; the meeting had taken its toll on us. How was I going to survive? The rage within was growing day by day like a malignant cancer and I didn't know how to control it. I later realised that my anger could kill me or someone else. I had to learn how to deal with it or it would destroy me. It was some five years before I finally was able to control the dark passenger who was making my life hell.

If I could advise anyone who was going through the murder of a loved one, it is to engage and work with the police. As hard as it may seem try and co-operate as it allows the police officers to be able to investigate without any obstruction and to quickly gather the information leading hopefully to the swift arrest and conviction of the person, or persons, who committed the crime.

Chapter 4

Jigsaw Pieces

It was a blustery freezing cold evening with the snow falling gently on the ground and it was time to go home. Freezing cold and slightly worse for wear Dean hailed down what he thought was a taxi. It was to be the most harrowing last journey that he was to take.

He was cornered like a frightened animal by four complete strangers and taken to a secluded beauty spot at Craibstone Golf Course on top of Elrick Hill in Aberdeen, where he was ordered out of the car at knifepoint. There they taunted, tortured and beat him unconscious and stripped him of his dignity by removing his clothes, leaving him to bleed and freeze to death, frightened and alone. His last thoughts were for his family. The Detective Inspector Alan Smith likened the boys to a pack of wild animals.

We don't know for sure, only what has been placed together by the police and the media of Dean's last moments. He was dropped off by his wife at 14.00 on the 3rd of April at the Criterion bar where he spent the next two hours chatting to the regulars until he and another man made their way to the Hen Hoose pub in the city centre. From there he frequented many bars until 22.00 when he finally made his way home. Rather the worse for wear Dean hailed down what he thought was a taxi. He unsuspectedly jumped in before he realised he had made the biggest mistake of his life.

As stated at the trial the four young boys held Dean captive with the intent of robbery and drove him to Howes Place where they robbed him at knifepoint. Not satisfied with that, they drove him to a car park at Elrick Hill where they repeatedly punched, kicked, stamped on and knifed him in the head and body. The four then stripped him of his clothes, abandoned him, severely injured, in freezing conditions and murdered him.

It only seems fitting that this chapter is dedicated to the man who investigated Dean's murder and whom I have nothing but admiration for. Due to the logistics and that I now live in Darwin, Australia, I asked Susan Mansfield a reporter for the Scotsman to undertake an interview with Detective Alan Smith about how they investigated and quickly secured a murder charge on Dean's killers, so in Alan's words:

I gave it a little thought coming down, because I suppose there's a danger that you become a little bit blasé about a crime as serious as murder when you are involved in a career where you are dealing with them on a reasonably regular basis. You've to guard against normalizing that kind of activity. And sometimes the very extreme cases jump out at you as being of interest in the public domain. But in terms of this particular case, it wasn't immediately clear that it was a murder, it wasn't clear at the outset what we were dealing with. It began to grow in the public imagination, in the sense that this wasn't somebody who was found slumped with a knife in his back and it was absolutely obvious from day one.

We had (a) the difficulty of establishing who the victim was – who is this man, his identity. The victimology and identity, that's the first thing. And then building up a lifestyle picture of this individual to try and identify, well, where does he work, where does he play, who are his friends, who are his associates. I think one of the first things you do, and accept, that in any situation in life, people have a public life, which is open to everybody, but people also have a private life which perhaps only close friends and family might see. But everybody also has a secret life, and that's maybe the parts that only the individual himself or herself will know about.

We believe that everybody has got that secret life, things that you would never confide, and typically if you can unearth some of that secret behaviour, that often leads you into an area where the answer lies. And I don't think Dean necessarily, I'm not saying that that type of secret life played out to lead him to where he was, but his lifestyle very much put him in that danger and that vulnerability which ultimately led to him jumping into a car with strangers, without properly assessing the situation. And the minute he was in, shut the door of the vehicle and drove off, that was it, his fate was sealed, from that point on.

When and how did you become involved?

So, on the day in question, that Dean's body was found, I was at a routine senior management meeting in Inverurie. It was mid-to-late afternoon and I was on route back to Aberdeen once the meeting was over and I got a phone call from my boss, the head of CID at the time, Jim Steven. Jim had picked up on an incident where a man's body had been found by a passer-by in a remote location on Elrick Hill. So immediately there were concerns before he phoned me. At that time I was his number two on CID, I was head of operations. So he asked me to go and basically make an assessment of what was there. It's not uncommon for bodies to be recovered in the open air, and usually what you find is it's suicide, or medical, but if it's medical it usually happens in front of people so it's an immediate response. But this is quite clearly a body that had been lying for some time, in the frost. So it wasn't a fresh body.

It was unseasonably cold, it was bitterly, bitterly cold. That was an immediate concern for me in terms of the crime scene, if it was a crime scene. En route I was thinking, *how are we going to preserve this?* Because

45

that's one of the big challenges if you've got a crime scene that's outside in inclement weather, you think, we're going to have to get some tents, we're going to have to get some protection up. So these were the type of things that were going through my mind. But this was well before we even knew for certain what we had. So when I arrived, I had just cut across from the A96 and I can't remember who I had with me, I met the uniform sergeant who had responded, a female.

We had a muster point, we didn't go straight to the actual location because clearly you don't want to contaminate anything. So we discussed the scene about one hundred metres from where the body was. So I didn't actually see the body, but that again is not uncommon, you absolutely restrict access to those who need it. The constable and the sergeant had been shown by the passer-by where the body was, and they had had the benefit of looking at the body visually. I remember the sergeant, who had previously been a detective constable, she was very good, and she had made an assessment that this was not a straightforward sudden death. Alarm bells were ringing, if you like, that he was all but naked and he was curled up in a fetal position.

But I think the most worrying thing was that she was describing what she thought might be a shotgun wound to the back of the head. There were marks of peppering of blood. She wasn't certain by any stretch of the imagination, but she was concerned that perhaps there was a shotgun-discharge type injury to the back of the head. So immediately, that's... But equally it's not uncommon for you to have suicides. But the very obvious thing was that there was no obvious weapon.

So we're at the scene, I'm being fed information by the sergeant, she's telling me that she's concerned about a possible mark at the back of the head. So I ask her to go back to the body and sketch what she can see. Sometimes we'll ask them to take a photograph with a mobile phone, but I didn't think that was appropriate at that time – because of the conditions or the darkness, nothing to do with intrusion. Or did I ask her to sketch it from her memory? That's what it was, I didn't want her going back unnecessarily, contaminating the scene again, so I asked her to sketch what she was talking about. She drew a diagram, peppered, she had a very limited view of what she saw, but she thought there were these peppered marks on the back of the head, which understandably could be explained away by maybe a shotgun. Again, I'm thinking, perhaps when we move the guy, is there going to be a gun, because he might have slumped over it? So I had a very open mind at that point in time.

But, given the circumstances, looked like quite a young man visually, from his body appearance, this wasn't like an old tramp or anything. It was beginning to get dark, it was getting to that time of day. So the first thing I did was I initiated a call-out for a full forensic team from the laboratory. We cordoned the area off. There was a thoroughfare where the body was. This was a public path, so we made sure we blocked that off top and bottom. so the body was hidden, concealed within bushes, very difficult to see.

Tell me about the circumstances which led up to that point.

Someone out walking, a chap out walking his dog I think, stumbled across the body and raised the alarm. Called 999 – *I've found a body*. I can't remember if the ambulance was called, typically they will send an ambulance anyway because you're not going to rely on a visual examination by a passer-by. There's a hierarchy which is quite interesting – the first thing is preservation of life, so you have to make absolutely sure that everything that can be done has been done for the victim. And if that means disturbing the evidence at the scene, that's a given. But once you establish that nothing can be done, you then move into the next hierarchy which is scene preservation and non-contamination. So that's where we were at.

There must have been an ambulance or a paramedic. We would have had a doctor. I can't remember if paramedics were qualified, at that time, to pronounce life extinct – they are now. I think at that time we had a doctor come along. The other thing we would do is call out our own pathologist. So Dr James Grieve, senior lecturer, you will know his history, he came and joined me at the scene. By this point I'd had the discussion –

48

I'd fed back to Jim, a phone call, look, this is nothing straightforward, we've got the body of a young male, in fetal position, potential injuries to the back of the head, looks suspicious. So I was designated the Senior Investigating Officer at that point, which is something you need to do in terms of who's got the authority, who's in control. The role of the SIO is a well-trodden path in terms of my experience at that time. So it's clear to everybody, then you start to put in place the layers.

The first thing is – let's get the scene controlled, the scene protected, and let's get some expertise in there in terms of the pathologist and the others – the chemist. You need to get the scene managed and protected. So James Grieve, pathologist, he came along, and I think Chris Ganacliff from the laboratory, he's the forensic scientist. So they come – but this is not going to happen immediately, though, it's a little slow-moving, so you've got this period of hanging about. And one of your early thoughts is media, what if, so again one of my calls would have been to our media officer, Susan Lumsden I think at the time, just a heads up saying, this is something that's going to burst, you're going to have to be ready to respond with some sort of holding press release, which typically would be, "Grampian Police are investigating the discovery of a body in wherever it is, enquiries are still at an early stage, et cetera," just enough to keep the lid on it. But that in itself creates a wave of activity which has to be managed. But as the SIO you really have to be able to delegate the responsibilities. The movies project this image that the man in charge or lady in charge arrive and go in and look at the body and the scene. The majority of murders I've dealt with I've never actually seen the body physically at the scene. I'll explain later how you do that.

Were you an experienced detective at that time?

At that time, I'd had... you go through as a detective, if your career path is what mine was in terms of CID, you go through training, you then go through training as a senior investigating officer, it's nationally accredited training.

(Describing the spot where the body was found) This was a bleak, remote hillside location. Something like 8-10 miles out of Aberdeen, maybe 5-6 miles. And it's an area that would be frequented by ramblers, dog walkers, Craibstone Golf Club abutted on to where the body was found. And so that immediate again, I was thinking, we're going to have to make an appeal. Because this is not a busy well-trodden area, but that can work in your benefit. Sometimes you would think the busier location means more witnesses, the more chance we have of finding out what happened, but it seems a remarkable thing that in a busy city centre location or a built-up area, something happens, and yeah there are lots of witnesses but nobody actually is watching, when they're in a city centre, they're going about their business. But when you're walking in a remote area, you're more alert to your surroundings, you're more likely to spot vehicles that are out of place. Because many of the people that frequent these areas, this is like a routine for them, so they might do it every Tuesday, or they might take their dog out every day at 11am. They're more likely to spot differences. Whereas in a city centre or built-up area, it's so chaotic people don't spot patterns. Sometimes that can play into your favour and it did here, because we had one witness who was a guy in a camper van he was able to tell us about the vehicle coming and going.

Very remote area, there were one of two dwelling houses in the area. One of the first things you would do in any investigation is house-to-house. Now this was more like a croft to croft than a house to house! But in the very early stages it's about assessing what we have, let's get the people in place, timescales, weather concerns. To maximise what you can achieve. Set realistic goals. The first thing we do, naturally, we go and scan missing persons. Have we got somebody reported missing? You'd expect friends and family of this young man by this time to have reported him missing (As is unclear at this point and should be checked). And that's what happened at a fairly early stage. I can't remember, I don't think he had been reported missing. But I might be wrong.

The reason I say that is, I think it took a while to join the dots as to who he was. It was the next day, I think, or later that night before we knew for certain who he was. And there was a carry on, there was angst with the family, either the Record or the Evening Express, I think it was the EE, ran the headline, *Tattooed Man*. One of the very obvious things, when we did get access to the

51

body, he had a very distinctive tattoo. I think it turned out to be one of his kids' names, you might need to check. I do remember the family were annoyed that Dean was being portrayed as being the tattooed man, it gave an impression of being a hooligan profile. You have to be very careful with families.

I remember with Arlene Fraser, we released a photograph of Arlene when she was missing, and it wasn't a very flattering photograph, it had been taken just after she'd been assaulted by Nat on a previous occasion, she was looking awful, but it was a good likeness. The family were furious because we were releasing a photograph to the media of their daughter, they'd had a series of glamorous photographs taken, that was what they wanted to put out. But the reality was that the man on the street wouldn't recognise her. So the family were keen to show her off at her best, whereas sometimes you've got to be more natural.

And these are the things you would never think about. One of the things from an SIO's perspective, you need to keep the family on side, you need to keep them united, you need to keep them updated, so you implant a FLO with the family.

But going back to the scene, pathologist arrived, swabbed, did what they do at the scene. Typically what they'll do at the scene is they'll photograph, video, swab as much of the body as they can before they move it. By the time they did they finish the procedure it's going to take a couple of hours. It's cold, it's dark, we've now got

52

lighting up, we've got some tenting, protection, tarpaulins up. Basic stuff but quite effective. We might have even had a tent, canopy, can't remember if that was in place at the time.

At some point near to midnight, 10pm, I think we got Dean removed from the scene and taken to the mortuary at police headquarters, Queen Street. Then there's a subsequent visual examination, not a post-mortem at that stage. What I had at an early stage was lots of superficial injuries, some sort of blunt force injury, or some sort of injury to the back of his head, which has led to significant blood loss. There were unusual cuts and abrasions to his knees and his fronts of his toes, which is consistent with somebody kneeling or crawling in a rough area. But there was also this mark like a cross on this thigh, a cut, this was a real curiosity because it didn't look like a random scratch. It was more like a scratch than a cut. This caused a little bit of concern because it looked like it could have been done by somebody. But there was no certainty about that.

Chapter 5

Tattooed Man

Were you were not expecting to be home for your tea that night?

No, I knew immediately that I was going to be (working) right through for the next 36 hours, almost certainly. I think I might have grabbed a couple of hours in the middle of the night to get a shower and a shave, but you were out very, very, early again, and you knew that was going to be a busy, busy day.

Because the media are now involved, there's speculation in the media that you have to deal with. So again, as an SIO you have to decide, are you going to delegate the media to one of your deputy SIOs, Willie Finlay in this case, who was a detective inspector. He was my deputy SIO. But my real priorities on day two, the day after he was found, is obviously who is he – by that time we knew who he was.

How did you establish that?

Can't remember. It was to do with the family getting in touch in response. I can't remember whether the media had gone out and said a body of a young man had been found, and they'd thought, *could that be Dean*, or had they reported him missing and we tied it up? I don't think that's the case, I have a sense that the family heard through the media and very quickly got in touch and said our son Dean is missing. Because I don't think it would have been wholly unusual for Dean to go out and not come back. So, if you think about it from a family point of view, Dean has been dropped off to go drinking in Aberdeen, and they know he drinks to excess, and they know he leads a chaotic lifestyle, pretty unstructured. So I think the fact that he didn't come home that night, that's not going to set them off on an alarm. I think they would have managed that through the family, phoning round.

He'd a mobile phone, obviously they would be trying to get in touch with him. So I have a sense that the family had heard that the police were investigating the discovery of a man's body. The tattoos, I think that's what triggered it, in fact. That must have been it, because we wouldn't have put out the appeal if we'd known who he was. We couldn't have known who he was before we were appealing for his identity, so they obviously hadn't reported him missing.

There was an appeal that went out for his identity and we used the tattoo as a point of reference, some sort of descriptive item that people might recognise. He hadn't got clothes, but (we could) say he was a young man in his thirties, and had quite an extensive tattoo in the neck area. That's what went out to the media, and that's what the family kicked off on. But that's also when we found out who he was.

Tell me about finding the identity of the victim through appeal?

That's a huge part of it, because once you have tried Missing Persons and found nobody we still had to get him identified, then formally identified by the family. I've a funny feeling it was Jo and one of the brothers. I don't think Carol went in. I wouldn't be there for that. But that would take place in the mortuary.

(Monday – went out drinking, body found on Tuesday afternoon) Something must have been seen in the paper, or late night news bulletin on Grampian or Northsound. Somebody somewhere in the family obviously joined the dots. It was either on Tuesday night, through the night, or the early hours of Wednesday morning that we really knew definitely that this was Dean Jamieson. And obviously from our point of view this was a big breakthrough.

But Jo didn't know until police came to the house.

I think we're missing something then. You'll be able to piece that together through them.

By the Wednesday morning we knew who he was, and some of the things that were going through my mind at that time – is this somebody who has been shot and their body's been dumped? That takes you into an area where you're thinking, OK, what are we speaking about here, this is criminality, could this be drug related? It's got that feel about it. At that time, coincidentally, in Aberdeen, we had been plagued by drug dealers coming up from the South of England and enforcing debts and wielding their brute force I was pretty sure it was only a matter of time before we ended up with something like this. So that was in my mind, could this be a local drug dealer who has been taught a lesson by some of these guys from down South. And so when we found it was Dean, very quickly that took me away from that theory, because he didn't fit the profile.

Obviously, very quickly you're going to check on his criminal record and his contacts with the police. You're going to run a full profile on this guy, his address, put that through, his family, immediate, we do what we call victimology, you're very quickly building up a picture of the profile of this guy, because that will help lead to probably what has happened. But here we had a picture of a guy who was a Kemnay loon, boy never really had any contact with the police beyond a few drunken interchanges which were of no real interest to me. He seemed to be a fairly straight, honest kind of fellow who liked a drink, and got himself into a bit of mischief here and there, but beyond that there were no warning signals in terms of drugs or crime.

But then, obviously the next thing is to piece together his known movements. So that then required you to go back and say, right, who last spoke to him, you check his mobile phone, do all those things to try to build up a history of a picture of his movements on the night in question. And that's done in pretty fast time, so that's like a dynamic ongoing thing on the Wednesday.

We had about 50 officers on the case by that time. The way you work on these things, you throw the resources at it, do what you have to do. We talk about the golden 24 hours after and that's when you've really got to put your energy into it, because that's the most productive and fruitful period of time. The longer you go on, the less energetic the investigation becomes, it becomes harder to jog people's memories, retain their interest, the media get jaded. So anyway, we had about fifty, I think, working on it. Many of them were involved behind the scenes, doing intelligence checks…

Tell me about contact with the family.

I remember that really well. I think it was probably one of the most interesting and potentially stressful (from my point of view) meetings that I had with a family because, typically, you want to meet with the family. They, obviously, are anxious. By this time you have embedded an officer with the family. So you've got a FLO, friendly face. The role of the FLO (Family Liaison Officer) is to provide support to the family, give them as much information as they can, not everything because stuff you still have to hold back. But also, there's a dual role, they're looking at the dynamics of the family, any tensions, any issues that might be of interest, because the majority, 95 or 98% of homicides are committed by somebody you know, either family, friends or acquaintances. It's very, very unusual to have a stranger homicide, and this is obviously what this turned out to be. But this is far and away the more remote possibility.

So you're trying to find out are there any family tensions, because of the type of lifestyle, Dean's separated, he's got four kids, there's a little bit of history of acrimony. We know he's a heavy chaotic drinker at times. All the ingredients, I suppose, were there, to give me enough concern perhaps – is there some sort of family tension?

Was he separated from Carol? Aye, he was actually. That was a curiosity to me, why his wife was dropping him off with money, in the town to go drinking. If they weren't physically separated, they weren't properly together. I think maybe he was a guy who would stay a night there, then maybe go home and stay a night with his mum, he was a little bit bouncing about I think. I think he had four children, and he was a good dad.

But at that point in time, (going back to the meeting), one of the responsibilities of the SIO is to meet with the family at as early a stage as possible, so you can introduce yourself to them, so they can see the whites of your eyes, and see who's actually dealing with the death of their son. That's going to be important. And also to just allow them to vent, allow them to ask questions, not all of them you can answer, but it's just cathartic, I think, to let them meet you. But the meetings, they're never straightforward, understandably. The emotions, you are in amongst… Remember, at this time, I didn't know, I was far from confident that we had a murder.

Because the pathologist's early and very strong hypothesis was this is a guy who was drunk, who had been out walking in the cold air, he had succumbed to hypothermia, and he had begun to strip off himself, which is symptomatic of hypothermia, and had perhaps stumbled and fallen into the bushes, causing the injuries. So he was very minded towards the death being non-suspicious. And I found that really hard because my instincts were different. It just didn't… there was part of that hypothesis that didn't hang together for me. We hadn't recovered all his clothes for example. There were things missing, his watch, his wallet, a Bench jacket. Again, he could have discarded them, it was an open area, we had extensive searches. That was another area that we did as well was search. I met with the family. I asked the FLO to arrange for me to meet with the immediate family at Bucksburn Police Station in the family suite, which is a good place to do that. That was arranged for I think 4pm on the Wednesday but it might have been the Thursday.

So here we are 2-3 days on and still we're not certain. Now I'm getting a lot of pressure as well from the media to declare what you are dealing with here. Is it a simple non-suspicious death, or it is a crime? And I couldn't answer that. That was a horrible situation to be in, because you don't want to look... because from a credibility point of view, it would be difficult for the family – difficult for the average man on the street to sit at home watching this senior detective going, well, we don't really know what we have here. He's either been killed or he hasn't. So I was very keen to get a definitive answer on what caused his death before we met the family.

Then, on the morning before I met the family, I got summoned to the mortuary by James Grieve, and he showed me some marks on Dean's arms, kind of pin marks, and he raised the possibility of this being drug-related. I don't think the family know this, but it's going to come out anyway. So he then introduced another scenario, that perhaps he was involved in heroin, which was worrying in two elements. Has he got a secret? Back to my question about the public, private, secret worlds. There are many professionals, probably within a couple of hundred yards of this room here, who are secretly abusing drugs and alcohol, and even family and friends don't know. So it's not inconceivable that that's possible, was he masking a drug habit with alcohol abuse, did this then introduce the drug theory? That took me back to my previous thoughts about the drug world, and maybe he has got a history. So that wasn't a great meeting. But the toxicology takes time, you can't rush it, so I wasn't going to get my answer as quickly as I needed it. So I left that meeting with my head in my hands, to be honest with you, now I've got another line of inquiry potentially.

James Grieve, I would say is one of the country's top pathologists, we had a fantastic working relationship, professionally. And he was doing everything he could to help me, but at the same time he can only do what he can do, he can't perform miracles. I often laugh when I watch detective programmes, you see the familiar scene where you've got the detective in the mortuary and you've got the pathologist, and within 10 minutes the pathologist is saying, 'I think it's probably somebody...' For a start, they are able to be specific about the time of death, well that's a fallacy. Being able to take the time of death to any (closer) than 6 hours. And then, "Somebody right-handed, standing at this location..." It doesn't happen like that. Or, if it does, I've never experienced it. It's more... I remember there was a murder at Inverurie, one of the first ones I've dealt with, it was a guy who worked in Inverurie Locos Club, he was the steward, him and his wife were tidying up at the end of the night and two young men came in and robbed them. He took chase after them, they stabbed him viciously and he was found in the street.

The point I'm saying is, even then the pathology, the difficulty we had in understanding, where was the knife, the entry point, it's sometimes very simplistic on the TV to wrap the whole thing up in an hour. But unfortunately these things create an expectation that you can't deliver.

So building up to the family meeting that day, I wasn't looking forward to the meeting. Not because I didn't want to meet the family, that is always something that's important, but I just knew there were going to be more questions than I could answer. And you don't want to be prevaricating with the family, you don't want to appear to be uncertain. You want to give an impression of credibility and confidence. You want them to go out the door thinking this is a guy who I think is going to get to the bottom of this, and do us justice, and if you lose the faith of your family, if they go out the door and think I don't know if this guy's got what it takes to do justice to what... because it's the biggest thing that's ever happened to them. You're not selling them double glazing, it's not like they could go elsewhere, this is who they've got. OK, they could ask for somebody else, but that never happens, very rarely happens, you don't want to be in that situation.

Chapter 6

Family Unity

I remember the meeting well, because typically the meeting with the family will be two or three of the family, usually two. The immediate – the husband, the wife, the father, the mother, it's very intimate. Now on this occasion, I remember the FLO coming in to say, "They're here."

I remember inquiring, "Who've we got?"

"Well, we've got Jo, the mother, the wife, the uncle, the brothers," there was about seven of them. I was horrified, I said "What on earth are you playing at?" This had the potential to dilute the experience for them, create all sorts of... But it was actually a positive. But I think it was during that meeting...

I was explaining to them... the first thing I do after I've introduced myself is give them a bit of my own background, so that they've got an understanding of where I've come from, what I'm about. I would just tell them my role is as Senior Investigating Officer. It's a role that you only acquire when you've got a certain level of experience investigating homicides. And so therefore you want to reassure them... if you're going to get heart surgery, you do not want it from somebody who hasn't done it before; you want to give them a little bit of reassurance. But more importantly, the team that you've got is a good team, that you've got solid support behind you, and that this is the biggest thing that's happening on the force at the moment, right now, the most important thing for Grampian Police is getting to the bottom of Dean's death. There is nothing happening anywhere in the Grampian Region right now that is more important than this, you are the absolute focus of the entire force. So that I think gets it into the context of, this isn't just another day at the office.

So you go through that, and then... you can only be one hundred per cent honest. Sometimes you can't tell them things you know, but I don't look upon that as being dishonest, that may be necessary to protect the investigation. Sometimes you've got – that cross, for example – if I was to reveal to the family this cross, apart from the fact that it would be distressing, if that information goes out through the family into the public domain, it becomes worthless as a piece of specialist knowledge at some later date. If you've got an accused who tells you something, reveals something to you in an interview that only someone there could know, evidentially that's powerful. If they could have read that in the Evening Express it's not worth a carrot, you know. So there are things you might want to hold back. That would be a classic example. And ultimately that was important, because one of them spoke about the bread knife swishing, which explained the injury.

Anyway, during the meeting with the family, I explained that we don't know for certain yet, despite extensive pathology and doing everything we can do, we don't know for certain yet what caused Dean's death. We're not even certain that it's criminality. These are difficult things to say, because understandably they had a very set agenda. You're a senior detective, there's a big hoo-hah publicly, it must be a murder. But I wouldn't be drawn into that. But what I did tell them, and what I told the media – don't worry what label we give this, whether I call it a murder, or whether I call it an unexplained death. It's not going to diminish or change the level of attention that it's getting. So don't think that maybe because we're giving this the label of an explained death, that you're going to get x number less detectives, x number less hours, it's just that we need to be careful what we call it at this point, looking ahead. So these are the things that we're telling the family.

I'm now telling them some of the things that we're thinking it might be. That perhaps Dean was walking home, or walking. Because if you think about it, as the crow flies, you've got Aberdeen here, Kemnay here, Elrick Hill was kind of equidistant. It wasn't away South, away to Stonehaven. If he'd been walking – so that was a theory. And remember, we don't know Dean, you know. But I remember at that meeting I had mentioned about him walking and perhaps succumbing to hypothermia, and I think it was his sister who just snapped back at me, and I can remember the expression that was used, *Dean wouldn't cross Union Street without using a taxi*. Dean wouldn't cross from one side of Union Street to the other without hailing a taxi. So the very notion that he was walking home, you can forget about it. So she just completely drove a horse and cart through that theory that we had some guy drunk and stumbling home. And that was really interesting, because that then created the biggest line of enquiry we had. And remember by this time we're beginning to piece together movements of Dean... we've done now a big media... who is he, where was he? We're getting phone calls about him being in the Criterion Bar with a guy who we're desperate to trace because we want to know who he was last with. This unknown male who he was last seen with in the Criterion Bar. We also had sightings of him on CCTV stumbling about, so clearly he was in the area of the city centre. And this was into the evening. We had a raft of inquiries.

Taxi drivers – we're bound to... he must have got a lift to where he was, either with somebody he knows and trusts, or something has happened to him and he's been dumped, or a taxi has taken him and for some reason has dropped him off. But it was interesting when the sister said, "No, no way, I don't buy that at all." It was useful. So a lot of good came out of that meeting.

What was the mood when you went in?

Quiet... there's always a tension. But it's mostly positive tension, in that they're just looking for answers. They know that you've got the most intimate knowledge of anyone, as to what's happened, they know you're in a position to control and determine the outcome of it. So they have to trust you. There has to be that bond. And it doesn't just happen, sometimes you've got to meet, and meet, and meet, sometimes you've got to work at that.

What happens if you don't have that?

I've fortunately never been in that situation, but you would choose your best supporting officer to perform that link role. So if you felt you weren't perhaps hitting it off with the family, or if they had doubts or suspicions about you as an individual, then obviously you're not going to come off the investigation unless there's good grounds for that. But you might delegate the role of dealing with the family to somebody who they get on with. Sometimes it's just a personality thing. But I was fairly encouraged by that first meeting, that despite the difficulties I seemed to engage quite well with Jo and the wife. I didn't come away from that thinking, *problems ahead.*

How did you get a sense of who will be the people you deal with most?

Jo. It was interesting because very quickly Jo was the family lead. I remember thinking how submissive and quiet the wife was. She didn't say very much.

What did you make of that?

I think my recollection is, they're separated, maybe she's just naturally quiet. What's her relationship with her mother in law, Jo? Is there a conflict there? I don't know. You just don't know, do you? Because they'll put on a united front for you, because they all want to meet you, that's why we've got a cast of thousands at this one, they want to meet the guy who's dealing with it. And so there are family differences... if you've got a crisis like a murder, you're not going to be getting exercised about who's going to Christmas dinner with who, but it's still down there, it will still bubble away, it will still surface. That's why the FLO is there, if they're living, pretty much twenty-four seven with the family, they'll start picking up on that before you would. But I didn't have any of that really.

Seven people came to meet you?

That's a random number, it was a lot, five or six or seven. But I just remember thinking this room is full of family, whereas normally you'd just be sitting down with two or three, and it would be much more intimate, much more engaging. This is more like briefing a team. And I remember falling out with the poor guy, the FLO, 'Never do that to me again, you've got to understand what you're doing here'.

What then is the routine after that – you've set up an incident room, which was at Bucksburn Police Station, you've got a dedicated inquiry team, you've got a structure in place. As a SIO the way I operated is, you'd have a briefing, say at 7am, and everybody would attend this. That might go on for perhaps an hour, and we would look at different areas of the investigation: where are we at with Dean's background, you would have teams (with different) responsibility, so you'd have those who were responsible for the scene, examining the scene, searching the scene. You'd have a team involved with the CCTV in the city centre. A team that was involved in house to house inquiries in the area. A team involved in doing background into Dean and anything that might have explain what's going on here.

You'd also have a team scanning intelligence that's coming in from informants and chitter-chatter on the airwaves of whatever in Aberdeen. Is there anything going on that's... anything that we should know about, people chatting. So you've got all this going on.

So each day, you have a structure, I'd have my topics and go through them. But it's important to do that in an open forum so that all the segments of the investigation team are privy to what's going on elsewhere, you want that cross-referencing, that's important.

You want to create an inclusive team who understand that the sum of the parts is going to lead to the outcome. So you don't have a few chosen detectives that you put on it – that's the myth of television again, it's never me that's going to solve this. It's going to be your team. This myth about – he's a great detective, he's cleared up x number of murders, that's a lot of nonsense. Naturally you've got a pride in how you do. But what I say, and it really is important, you want to have the best people you can get working on your team, but you can create this (atmosphere of) inclusion and sharing knowledge, and we'd do that 7am and before we finish at night, 6pm. Twice daily, we'd have everybody into the room, this is may be 60-70 people, exchanging ideas, it was really productive. So I always enjoyed the briefing and debriefing because it was an opportunity to motivate the team as well.

If you've got an inquiry that's in the early stages, motivation is simple, but if you've got an inquiry that goes into days and weeks and months and – as it was with Arlene Fraser – years, it's very difficult to keep that intensity going. At this stage, no problem. But we still didn't know what had killed him. And I can't simply go out and… it's not my decision what goes into the media. I can suggest what I want to put out to the media, but everything I have would have to go to the procurator fiscal to get authorised. And at this point in time, I was absolutely forbidden from talking about murder, suspicion of criminality, it was very very tight what I could say. So I really found it difficult doing some of the TV interviews. I remember in particular a guy from Reporting Scotland, doing an interview at the back of the police station in Bucksburn, and he was basically saying, come on, you're two, three days on, surely you must be able to say is this a murder or is it not. I was having to hold the position and say no, sometimes you need… I remember coming away from these ones really feeling that this wasn't fantastic, it was beginning to frustrate me that we didn't know. I couldn't believe that we were three days into it and we didn't have a definitive yes it's a crime, or no it's not.

And there was a sense of time ticking?

Yeah, but you balance that with the sense that, just because we didn't know what killed him, there was still a huge momentum of investigation going on, so we weren't losing anything. But I was craving a break, one way or the other, to say this is what we had.

We had probably taken the city centre sightings of him as far as could. We'd tracked him in pubs. We knew he'd been refused entry to a couple of clubs, we knew he was generally down in the area of the harbour, that neck of the woods, so again that part of the investigation you're naturally thinking... (phone rings)

Day four we're still not certain what's occurred, and we're still curious to understand how he got from the city centre to where he is (where his body was found). We've dismissed the possibility that he's gone rambling, so you're left with stranger, a taxi, but then why would a taxi drop him off? And then you think, did he have enough money, has he perhaps been lippy, has he offended the taxi driver and got turfed out and then he's gone wandering. So these were all real possibilities. But it did seem a very strange remote location, even for a taxi driver it was unlikely. The route for a taxi driver was the A96, so even if there had been some sort of dispute over the fare, we just didn't think it was probably credible that a taxi driver would waste time driving the necessary 15 or 20 minutes to this location to dump him. Would he not just dump him in a lay by on the A96... he would want to get rid of him quickly, just get shot of him. So that didn't... There were a lot more questions than there were answers.

The family gave me a lot of breathing space. You could have expected the family by this point to be putting pressure on me for answers. Yes, they were naturally curious, but they weren't... you're looking for signs of hostility or animosity or frustration. But they were very good, they understood we were doing all we could, very supportive.

And then, the house to house, it was more like croft to croft (in that area). We thought we'd got a break, because there was a property, a house, a matter of several hundred yards from where Dean had been found, maybe a conversion. We found that the police had been called to a disturbance, a noisy party, on the night that Dean had gone missing. And that then introduced a line of inquiry, has Dean somehow met in with somebody in Aberdeen and been invited to this party. Has he gone to the party, has he been chucked out of the party because he hasn't behaved himself, that explains why he's been found a short distance away. Has something happened in the house, has there been a fight? So that became a focus for a chunk of time. I'm thinking maybe a day or two.

So we had all the people who were at that party to interview. There were no obvious signs... somebody had called 999, called the police about a noisy party, or somebody within the party (had called), and when the police officers attended things had just fizzled out, there was nothing to say that Dean was there or thereabouts. It was one of these lines of inquiry that you get in any murder investigation... unless you're very... if you get a... I would say easily 80% of murders clear themselves before the police arrive, or before the detectives arrive.

So when you arrive at a murder, you've got a body, you've got a clear cause of death, witnesses are telling you what happened, and more often than not you've got somebody in custody. So it's more a question of knitting it together... it's not a whodunit. This was a proper whodunit, not even whodunit, we hadn't got to that stage yet, it was still – what is this? So in terms of frustration, it was without question the most frustrating investigation I've had from the point of view of – how can we not know? Are we missing something?

It was beginning to cause me a significant amount of anxiety that I couldn't give the public, couldn't give the media, couldn't give the family, couldn't give my own inquiry team a real direction to go in. And so what you're doing then is you're running an investigation like a snow plough, you're trying to keep everything, trying to gather as much as possible just in case. Whereas if you've got a very specific set of circumstances you can narrow the focus of your investigation right down into areas, and that makes it much more productive, much more effective. It was slow, it was slow, it was cumbersome, frustrating for everyone.

Chapter 7

The Big Break

So, how did we get the break? (seems to be asking himself).

That came through chit-chat in Northfield between the community. Snippets of information were being leaked out by various youngsters, speaking to youngsters. It's funny, if it happened now I think it would have come out on social media. I think if that had happened 10 years later, like now… there wasn't that social media interaction. But that's an interesting dynamic to policing, full stop.

But anyway, I'm in my office and Martin Mackay who was my detective inspector in charge of the intelligence section, the section of the investigation that was looking at what's being said, what are informants speaking about, is there talk in the pubs and the clubs and the streets that we should be picking up on. So it's more like a scanning of the community, informants – every police force has informants that work within the criminal sub-underworld. If you've got something like this they'll be tasked, they'll be taken in and told look, go forth and try and hear what you can. But that's not how this came about. It came about through chit-chat amongst minor groupies of criminals.

So Martin Mackay showed me a piece of paper, it was an intelligence report that came in from the Northfield area, submitted by a police officer who had been made aware by a member of the public that apparently there had been a party, or some sort of gathering of youngsters, in Northfield the night that Dean had gone missing. Some named guys were bragging about doing somebody in, picking him up in their car, that they had videoed it, that they'd given him a hiding and dumped him away out in the middle of nowhere. I remember reading it and thinking, OK, could this be something or nothing.

So a police officer had heard it?

Yeah, that's how randomly it had come in to the… that's not uncommon, that's why I'm saying, when you solve these things it's not through Poirot detective-type activity, it's usually going to come to you from… the important thing is to have a structure in place in the investigation so you're going to structure all these things, so you're giving yourself the best opportunity.

So that could have been an officer doing something else?

Absolutely, it could have been a community officer in Northfield who just happened to be in a house on an inquiry, completely unrelated, and randomly somebody said, "I heard a story on the grapevine last night that these young boys were in a house and they were bragging about beating up some young lad and dumping him." That is how it came to… That then became our main line of inquiry.

I was thinking, *could this be just bullshit, for want of a better word.* Because you do get kids who want to jump on the back of something and try to impress people with bragging rights. I think in every murder investigation I've had, you get at least one person who comes in off the street wanting to admit it. For the notoriety, to get the centre of attention. Idiots are dangerous. And you get the same with witnesses. We get witnesses who come forward who are actually… There's an axis we look at for witnesses, willing and unwilling or able and unable. If you've got a witness who's willing to help you and able to help you because they've seen it, they're the prime witness. But the dangerous witness is the one who's willing to help you but unable.

You might think, why might that happen, but it does. It's a phenomenon that you get where witnesses will come along and try and ingratiate themselves to the police by telling them things they might want to hear. So what I'm getting at is, this was one of these situations where you think, we need to test the veracity of this, we need to do more. So then the strategy was – we had some names, but you don't just go and knock on their door, because you don't want to frighten them off, and again, it would be a myth that you see in films – if a suspect for a murder is identified at an early stage, sometimes it might be one, two, three days before you actually... arrest them.

The first thing you'll do then is you'll do the same profiling on the suspect as you'll do on the victim. So you want to do as much as you can before you actually... (approach them) and quite often that will involve things like we did here, we'll put them in behind surveillance. We've got some named suspects, so when you get the names Leslie and Cowie and Paton coming into the frame, very quickly you think, hang on, these guys have got the profile that might match this. And then you learn, when you dig more, that actually one of them – and I can't remember which one – had come into contact with the police for using his car as an illegal taxi. And then you start thinking, hang on, now, now this is beginning to excite you, because you're thinking, could this be an explanation why Dean went into the vehicle, and [they] took him to this location.

So, all of a sudden you can see the spotlight of the investigation really homing in here. So we know that these guys are capable of derailing trains, they've got that thuggery about them.

Were they names you'd heard before?

Oh yeah, all of these were well known in the Northfield area. What would you call them? I suppose, if I was describing them… they're not career criminals in any sense. They're young guys, but they were all young men who had a significant history of criminality already, they'd had a life of coming into contact with the police, with escalating levels of violence. I think one of them had maybe done a year in prison for assaulting somebody. So they had that, it's an interesting mix. And so… how did we play that out?

Again, we couldn't go into this hornet's nest, if you want to call it that, because you don't want to give them the slightest inkling, they would be spooked, that's going to cause them to scatter. So you need to then play a strategic cat and mouse game, where you do as much evidence gathering as you can in the background. OK, so what cars were they using just now, would that explain the vehicle that he was taken out in? So you want to identify the car.

Ultimately, that's going to be a huge forensic capture for you. If I can get Dean Jamieson's DNA, or any transfer of fibres on their vehicle, then that could be the physical link to them, and ultimately… So before I jump in, I need to know what vehicles have they got access to, what vehicles are they using.

So we put them under surveillance, each of them, and that's a really intensive, resource-intensive business. Again, there's mythology about how you follow somebody. It takes a minimum of ten to twelve officers per person, with three to four, maybe five vehicles, to perform one surveillance on one individual. You've got to be able to follow them about in vehicles or on foot, obviously without risking any chance of them seeing you. There are well documented techniques on how that's done, but what I'm saying is, the point of it is that you need a huge amount of resource to do that.

The police, Grampian, – had one surveillance team, so they were obviously dedicated to it, but then I had to call on support from the Scottish Crime Squad in Glasgow, and other forces, to come in and provide that level of surveillance. So really now we're into what I would call the dynamic, intensive (phase of the investigation)… we've got the bit between our teeth now. And for the first time I'm thinking, actually I'm thinking, you know something, it's now making sense for me as an SIO.

What are you looking for in a murder?

Well, the first and foremost thing is, have you got a motive? Nobody kills somebody without a motive, and that's going to be either anger, revenge, financial, maybe romantic, relationship, there's something, passion, you know. But the obvious case here is robbery, because that's the kind of makeup of them (these guys). We know from the profile we've filled already that they've got taxis. Very early on we were thinking, has he been the subject of a robbery, ended up in a taxi, either fallen out with them and got a doin', (doin' is a Scottish slang word for beaten up) or hasn't had the money to pay? That's what you're thinking. Or has he been robbed and dumped or something. Or do they know him? Is there something in his past life which has brought him into contact with any of the three of them? Probably less likely, but still you couldn't discount it. So these are the kind of things you're thinking of.

We had four names at that stage, Colin Cowie, Colin Stewart – he was the guy who turned Queen's evidence. And also, one of them, when they picked him up, Phil Eddie, he gets dropped off at the house, and one of the others comes out and joins them. There was a kind of transfer… we didn't know that till… that was much further down the line.

(So to put surveillance on each of them – you're going out on a limb and saying 'this is the answer')

Before I made a decision to deploy that, I had to justify that, and you can imagine the associated costs with that.

Because a murder investigation isn't open ended in terms of budget.

One of the roles of the SIO is to manage the budget. So you've got 50 officers, you can't have them working 18 hours a day because they're going to drain your budget in over time, so you have to be very fiscal minded in terms of how you spend the money here. So if we get into this level of resourcing, you're talking thousands, tens of thousands. OK, you don't measure an investigation by – that's your budget and if you go over your budget that's the end of the investigation. But as SIO I would have to justify expenditure, and I would have to be able to – if I had to go back and get more, I would have to… So part of the role of the SIO is a business manager, it's not just about going and catching the bad person. It's a tricky role, because you've got people's personalities, team dynamics, you've got the logistics of where are you working out of. -

Feeding the guys, you know, you might think that's… but you know guys out searching out on Elrick Hill, have they got the correct clothing? I remember we had to buy waterproof clothing, jackets for the officers because it was so cold. These things are necessary and they're important, but it's not really what you want to be doing. I don't want to be signing off on an invoice for 20 Berghaus jackets when I could be concentrating on… but that's the kind of things you need to be… You're project managing the whole thing. But by this time, now, this is exciting…

How were you able to justify bringing in surveillance teams?

It was easy, because we need to know who these people are, we need to know the vehicles they've got access to, we need to know who are they – are they interacting with each other? But more importantly, who else are they interacting with? Where are they staying?

These guys don't live like you or I would live at an address, they'll have an address, but they live a gypsy lifestyle, they move about. They might stay 2 or 3 nights in one part of the scheme – they're very much Northfield-based. Where are they staying at night, so when it does come to the arrest phase, we know where to go and get them. What vehicles are they using, or have access to, so we can maximise everything we can do by way of forensic capture. Who are they associating with, so we can go and use the friends and associates as potential witnesses, because the likelihood is that they will be the people who have been shown this video, if such a video exists.

So we did our surveillance. I think we struggled to find one of them, one of them had cleared off down to Glasgow. Now I can't remember the sequence of events but we arrested one of them, and some of them handed themselves in. And it was like a pack of cards, and that is exactly what you would expect to happen. So there was a really intense period of about 24 hours, Susan, when we started hoovering up all these guys. And the people around them. And there were teams of detectives tasked with interviewing them. And this became our main, our only line of inquiry. So we threw all our eggs into this basket, but the more we went down that [road], the more confident we became.

Suddenly we were getting very strong stories from associates who had been taken in, young, fifteen year-old girls who had been in the house. I remember recalling them speaking about – I had been doing a press interview on North Tonight, just a routine thing on the news at night, and she'd been in the room with one of them, I can't remember which one. And as soon as the thing came on TV he was jumping up and down saying 'that was us, that was us'. So we were confident that we were getting into… There was talk of this video, and a few people had been shown this video of this guy getting… So that again, important from our point of view, we wanted to capture that, we didn't want them to dispose of that video. They did, as it happened, we never ever recovered that video. We recovered the phone but we couldn't recover the video.

And so over the period of twenty-four hours, we got the guys into custody. I'd be absolutely telling you a lie if I said I remember at what stage, but it began to crumble like a house of cards. They all began blaming each other and… What then typically happens if you've got a group of young guys involved in the one crime with varying degrees of responsibility, they will begin to start positioning themselves to diminish the blame on themselves, and promote others as if things were their idea. But we had certain areas of physical evidence that we wanted to recover, obviously the vehicle was one – which we did, we were able to recover the phone, we were able to recover the breadknife. We think we got the breadknife, but it had been cleaned, there was never any DNA or traces of DNA on the breadknife. It showed that either we had the wrong knife or it had been thoroughly cleaned.

We had a lot of circumstantial evidence, we had evidence of them bragging about it, we had evidence of them blaming each other. So the whole thing began to unravel for them. That must have been the weekend, because they all appeared in court on the Monday, all four them, charged with murder.

Chapter 8

In the Wrong Place at the Wrong Time

Was the charge satisfying?

Oh yeah, fantastic. There is no feeling like getting to the bottom of it, it's a euphoric feeling. You've achieved your objective in terms of your own professional objectives, but also you're able to go to the family and say we've done what we said we would do. And you're able to give them some… That meeting with the family after it is always going to be emotional. It's a strange time, you get a lot of high fives and fists punching. It's quite an energetic thing, there's a lot of back-patting, and thank you, all this type of thing. That all happened.

Did you interview any of the suspects yourself?

No, that's not something you would do. That's not what happens, you've got a structure. So, you're up here, as Chief Investigating Officer, and you've got your different areas, and each of those areas you'll probably have a detective inspector responsible. One of the areas is interviews, and they'll have teams to do the interviews which feeds back into the rest of the investigation. So, again, back to the myths, I never set eyes on Dean Jamieson until he was in the mortuary, I didn't go near him at the scene. I never set eyes or spoke to any of the accused, never went down to the cells to see them or speak to them.

Why wouldn't I do that? Because there's no need to, that's not really what I'm there for. What are the risks of doing that? You're just introducing the potential for them to, perhaps, make it personal. So you depersonalise it – what you feel towards them. I remember giving the post-trial press conference and speaking about them acting in akin to a pack mentality. Ultimately that's what this was. I think, these four guys went out, they didn't go out to kill, I don't think they realised they'd killed him, because the injuries.

There was a pathologist appeared for the Defence and he spoke openly and candidly about the fact that Dean Jamieson's injuries were never life-threatening. Had he been afforded medical intervention at an early stage he'd still be here today. This wasn't hard work, these were the kind of injuries you'd see in an A&E

department any Friday night, a couple of stitches and he would be out. What it was, was the profuse bleeding coupled with the exposure to the cold. The length of time that he was isolated out there. It was the sum of the parts that killed him. If they had summoned an ambulance to the location, even if they'd left and just made a 999 call – and I've seen that happen before – you could have ended up with it being just no more than an abduction and an assault.

For the robbery – it was pathetic – amounted to a watch, a jacket, a pair of trainers, this was low level, juvenile type criminality, which had a completely disproportionate outcome because they exposed him to that danger. Are they murderers? Not intentionally, I don't think. They're thoughtless, they're all of these things, adjective-wise, but I don't think there was ever an intent to kill Dean Jamieson.

How does that work, two of them got murder convictions?

You've got to look at the definition of murder, I suppose. And if it's an act so reckless with a complete disregard for life that takes it into the... it's either an intent to kill, or an act so reckless – I'm trying to remember my definitions now – or an act so reckless with a total disregard for life, and that's what this came into. The beating him up, the stripping him, all that humiliation, what they did to him was just awful. They absolutely humiliated him, he was stripped, he was pulled around, he was made to perform, it was all these things that combined to make it... I think when I reflect on this now, what makes this case, I suppose, unique in a sense, for me, is that there were so many opportunities for this not to happen. If he hadn't been out drinking in Aberdeen that day, and been dropped off, if he'd stayed at home in Inverurie or Kemnay and gone to the pub, he'd still be alive. If he hadn't got so drunk that he wasn't really fully in control of himself, perhaps he would have thought twice about getting into a strange car. Why did the warning bells not ring? Whenever do you get into a taxi with 3 or 4 people in it? There are so many things, I think, that his number, if you like, was up that day.

The pathologist's initial theory was that it was hypothermia – did he come back later with a different theory?

Yeah, that's a good point. Once we got to the point where we had a better understanding of what had happened... So once we'd interviewed them, and knew that he'd been picked up down the harbour drunk, that they'd seen him and said, 'There's a victim'. They were out prowling, is how I would put it, they were like predators. They were out that night – not looking to kill somebody, but to rob somebody. He was the chosen victim. So when he was in the car, he was... And one of them even spoke about the interview guy being a nice friendly guy from Kemnay, cheery, happy-go-lucky kind of individual. So there was obviously a period of time on that journey when it was quite chatty. At some point, that changed, and it must have been then that Dean realised, 'Hang on, this isn't good'.

But once we'd found out through the various interviews that he'd been taken out, and ordered to strip off. We knew there was this breadknife on the go, and we had one guy speaking about slashing, and hitting him on the back of the head with the knife, we knew all that. Then what I do is I go back to James Grieve and I say, 'OK, now I've got another hypothesis here'.

So I would then tell him, this is what I think might have happened, is this possible? And every time it's yep, yep, that would explain this cross, the swishing of the knife, that would explain the serration. You've got a knife that you're showing him – could this be the weapon? – absolutely. Could the marks on his knees be caused by him crawling naked on a rough stony surface? Yes, absolutely. The fact that the soles of his feet were completely clean and devoid of any injury. That he was never at any point standing up, he was always either kneeling down or crawling. And so you're building up a picture all the time of this pitiful character, drunk, disorientated, bleeding, frozen, panicking, all of these things going on.

I suppose the wickedness, Susan, comes out of the fact that at some point these guys must have thought, 'Hang on, we've gone too far here'. You would have hoped that one of them would have had the moral courage to either try to stop it or at least go back and say,'Shit, this is bad'. In fact, worse than that, they went back and bragged about it.

We did hear as well that one of them, I can't remember which one, went out the following morning to see if he was still there. Because they didn't think they'd killed him. It was only when it came out on the news. They thought he'd probably managed to get himself on his feet and away. But they didn't find him because he was hidden away in the bushes, they didn't go and really look.

And then you've got the trial, and all the dynamics of the trial, and then you've got the family to deal with after the trial. But by that point in time, October, it's an emotional time. One of them gets released on the basis that he turns Queen's evidence. That's always a tricky one, for the family, again. Adrian Cottam was the prosecutor, Adrian's very good, he explained the rationale behind that to the family, they weren't consulted on it but they were kept in the loop. I had a very similar thing happen with Arlene Fraser, I keep talking about that but again, big trial, one of the guys turned Queen's Evidence at the eleventh hour. It was the only way we were going to get a conviction.

So sometimes you have to trade a little. And so the pay off, the trade off is, you've got four guys, we believe this guy played a far lesser role, if anything he was part of the pack but he was at the back of the pack, dragged along by the aggressors. But here's a guy who will be able to go into the witness box and testify against and name the three guys which is probably going to help to secure the conviction, because this is really just a circumstantial case. We didn't have eye witnesses, other than themselves, which is always dangerous. And we didn't have the phone. If I remember, we had a very loose, weak DNA link between one of them, the guy's boxer shorts, one of them had been holding him up by the boxer shorts, they'd ripped into three parts. But every time a little bit more came out you were able to build up this picture – just a horrific picture of what would have been his last few hours.

Did it shock you?

I think every murder has an impact on you in different ways. Sometimes it can be the age of the victim, you know, a young victim or a vulnerable victim. That can compound the feeling. Or if you've got a particularly horrific set of circumstances in the way that the murder's actually carried out. Extreme violence or extreme torture, these things accentuate. And I think in this case what struck me was how callous these guys had been, in the sense that they'd picked up this guy as a victim of robbery, and they'd allowed it to continue beyond robbery into frenzied pack-attack on this decent young guy who was a vulnerable drunk, and probably offered little or no resistance because he wasn't able to.

I think that was the overriding thing, they kind of mocked him, there was a bit of... it's difficult to put it into words. You wanted to catch them badly, you know, and once you caught them and found out how they'd done it, you really wanted to convict them, you wanted them to pay for it. And I think the fact that Sean Paton is now back out walking the streets of Aberdeen, no wonder the family might feel that they haven't had the justice they maybe deserved. I remember Jo giving an interview when he was released, and she was very very bitter and vitriolic about the Scottish justice system. And I can't blame her, I suppose, is six years enough? For a young guy who's out before he's thirty. Doubt it. So it's a hard one.

His conviction was manslaughter?

He was on manslaughter, again, because obviously the Crown had a view that he took a lesser role in the whole thing. I find it hard to carve out that level of responsibility. I think, you know, they must have all at some point hit a tipping point and thought, 'Yeah, this is a good idea,'or,'this is OK'. There's no doubt that Colin Cowie and Kevin Leslie, who are strong characters, were leaders of the pack, which is probably why they got twenty and eighteen years respectively.

Was it a premeditated murder? No. They didn't set out to kill him. It was a stranger murder, it wasn't premeditated. I suppose it's a bit, what would you say, a classic example of being in the wrong place at the wrong time. But in terms of vulnerability, he put himself into that situation. It would be very easy to sit and be pious and say, 'Well, if he hadn't had so much to drink, and if he didn't put himself down to the harbour area, and if he hadn't got into a taxi,' but that's not life. You can't excuse what was done because he was drunk and a bit reckless. I suppose that's where Jo's coming from when she says, 'He's not an angel, but he didn't deserve that.'

There's not much more to the story than that.

You must have got quite a picture, by the end, of Dean himself?

My impression of Dean was that he was a family guy. He was, I hesitate to say, dysfunctional, I think chaotic in his lifestyle, he loved a drink. I would imagine often at the expense of his marriage, in the sense that he was a bit of a party animal, a hail-fellow-well-met, in a pub he was quick to strike up a conversation. He wasn't violent.

Could he be argumentative? I think so; he could be cheeky. He could be all of these things that could potentially get a slap around the head or a bloody nose, not abducted off the street, driven to his death, tortured and humiliated and left to die, that's the difference. I think it's the extreme measures that led to his death that set this case aside. If he had done something to annoy these guys, if he had done something to agitate or anger or infuriated these guys, whilst it would never justify it, it might explain why they did it. But all the indications from the interviews are that, right up until the death, he was trying to, even when he was out of the car and having to strip off, befriend them; he was trying to get them to stop doing this. "What are you hoping to achieve? Take what I've got." He wasn't fighting back, he wasn't kicking in the back of the car, he wasn't shouting and arguing and resisting. Right up until the last moment, he was pleading with them to see sense and stop doing this. He knew, and his defence mechanism wasn't to fight back, that it was probably best to try and endear himself to them and get them to rationalise what was going on and stop it. Does that make sense?

And I suppose, in some ways that makes me feel a little bit sorry for him, because you get this picture of this pitiful character, trying to wriggle out of a situation where he must be thinking, how did I get into this? Who are these people? What have I done?

That's one of the things I remember saying at a press conference, that I would think that night Dean Jamieson sobered up very quickly in the back of that car. I think irrespective of how much drink he had, I think he would have sobered up very quickly when he realised what was going on. Maybe the family would like to think he was so drunk, maybe that's the memory they should have, but my own personal view is that he would have been pretty compos-mentis; confused, disorientated and I think aware his life was in danger

It had an impact on the community; people stopped walking their dogs in that area, they saw it as stained, tainted. They're not going to walk their dog past the spot where a guy was killed. There's more than one dimension to that investigation.

People who jump on the thing and say, *why was he in the pub?* People say, *well, he deserved it, he was out drunk, away from his wife, he should have been at home* – people have different agendas, you've got to protect him and the family a little bit.

It was the most remarkable, ill-fated drinking session that anyone ever had.

There would be two hundred to three hundred guys out in Aberdeen on any given night, lone males with the intention of getting drunk, having a curry and going home to their beds. That's what makes me think the moral brigade can take a running jump – the randomness of this.

Chapter 9

Liaison Officers

Where the police investigate a death they have a positive duty to communicate with the bereaved family. Normally a Police Family Liaison Officer (FLO) has this role. Police Family Liaison Officers are experienced police officers who have been specially trained to enable them to act as such when necessary. They acknowledge that they may not be able to make things better but can at least not make things worse.

The Family Liaison Officers is primarily an investigator whose task is to gather material from the family in a manner which contributes to the investigation. They inform and facilitate care and support for the family who are themselves victims, in a sensitive and compassionate manner in accordance with the needs of the investigation. They need to gain the confidence and trust of the family, thereby enhancing their contribution to the investigation.

The trauma associated with a sudden unexpected tragedy places the family of the victim under immense personal pressures at a time when the needs of the investigation will make heavy demands for detailed information. Sensitivity, compassion and respect for the family's needs and requirements must underpin the approach to gathering material. The initial priority must be to establish communication with the family as soon as practicable in order to furnish them with any information that they require, in accordance with the needs of the investigation.

It struck me then how compassionate Adrian and Faye were, both trying to be as sensitive as possible but knowing that they had to try and get as much information as possible. Time was of the essence. Research shows that the more information you have early on in an investigation, the better the results. They were soon to become regular visitors to our home for the next few months. They worked long and arduous hours well into the evening trying to build a case. They were the faces that we would see when we got up and when we went to bed. They had no social life for the next few weeks and we tended to rely on them for information and support. They protected us from the media as much as they could, but it became a necessary evil. They were like family.

A conversation later that I had with both Faye and Adrian was that through our relationship they felt they got to know Dean and this helped them with the investigation. Part of their role was to obtain full victimology, lifestyle and behavioural information. They were very experienced in how they were able to glean this information in such a sensitive manner. They went above and beyond the call of duty for that, us as a family are eternally grateful. They attended the trial with us as well as assisting us in court. It is important that people who are victims or family of a murder investigation that you engage and work with your FLOs to get the best results. It makes it easier on the family.

Faye and Adrian put us in touch with Victim Information and Advice Services, for when the investigation is over and the case is heading for trial you are accompanied by the officers of the procurator fiscal office who are meant to provide you with the information regarding court proceedings and what is happening. However, as a family we felt that the service was inferior compared with the FLOs and lacked the compassion and professionalism that they showed us. Luckily for us, Faye and Adrian were allowed to accompany us throughout the trial and they even attended on their day off, such was their commitment to the family.

In the early days when Dean was murdered we were provided with a book that provided you with information to help support you when you have been affected by murder. I remember phoning the victim support agency written in the book and enquiring about what they could provide the family. They said they could provide counselling, emotional and practical support, but there is a waiting list of six months. Great, not much use to us as Dean's children required the help now, not in six months. This was exceptional circumstances. As a social worker I have access to a list of support agencies so after a few calls and persistence I was able to access counselling for the children. I spoke to the agency about a support package and was one available and they replied that they were working on one. So I guess in my experience the only people that we could count on were the FLOs.

Liam, Dean's oldest son, wanted to attend court, but at age nine we thought it would be too traumatic for a child to endure and listen to the horrific stories that would be read out in court. It was bad enough for him to hear it on television and read about it in the newspaper. He wanted to know who would be attending and what court was like. Adrian told Liam that he would take him to court to see what it was like and he could ask all the questions that he wanted to ask. You see, Liam had wanted to ask the people who killed his father why they hurt his dad and took him away. As I said, above and beyond the call of duty.

Adrian received permission from the Procurator Fiscal to take Liam to the Stonehaven Court and spend some time in the courtroom where Liam sat in the judge's seat and asked Adrian the questions that he so desperately needed answered. Adrian answered as best he could. It was the best therapy session ever. Adrian spent the time with Liam and with much patience was able to put a little boy's mind at rest as best that he could and it made a massive difference to Liam's emotional wellbeing.

For the next three or so weeks, until they had enough information that could help support Dean's case in court, Adrian and Faye would arrive at 9.00 a.m. amid the chaos of a roomful of people searching for answers. Cups of tea and biscuits were offered and I remember one day after quite an exhaustive interview Faye and Adrian were working through their lunch hour. My mother, god bless her, was keeping herself busy making sandwiches and when she offered some to Adrian he politely declined. My mother, a small but very authoritarian woman, insisted that he take some and we could only laugh at this small woman bullying this big man into taking sandwiches like a small school boy. We often laugh about it to this day.

Faye and Adrian also had to undertake the job of accessing as much information on all the family members in the household. These details must be obtained in a sensitive and professional manner while compiling the family tree. This provides the FLOs with a clear picture of the family structure. I was aware that the FLOs were trying to balance the needs of the family with the requirement to gather material and preserve the integrity of the investigation. They were interested in Dean's lifestyle, family, friends and associates where he hangs out how often, the questions endless. They said that it may hold the key to identifying witnesses, suspects or other vital information.

I remember from the onset asking the police if we could attend the location where Dean had been found and they said that it was a crime scene and we would not be allowed to attend for some time. We spoke to Faye and Adrian and they managed to get us permission to visit where he was found at a time when it didn't interfere with any forensic investigation. As a family it was important for us to visit the scene. We were in a state of shock and at the time asked questions but could not take it in; they were able to fill in the blanks. It is vital that trust is established with your Liaison Officers to make for a better working relationship. If Faye or Adrian were unable to answer any of our questions, they were open and honest and made an assurance to try and find out. Sometimes they were able to, but at other times they had no answer. They took care not to make any unrealistic promises to us.

Dean's murder generated enormous media attention and Faye and Adrian were aware of the animosity that existed in the early days between the family and the media but knew that they needed the media to get access to any information that the public could hold. They very gently sat the family down explaining the need to exploit any investigative advantage from family exposure to the media coupled with the need to protect the family from unwarranted media intrusion

The family held a meeting with the FLOs and we discussed the need to develop and agree the police and family media strategy. We were careful that any information that was provided did not adversely impact on the investigation and we as a family were encouraged to work with the media to ensure that they remained on our side and assisted with the investigation. We put our faith in the hands of the Family Liaison Officers.

Grampian Police worked hard at bringing the four accused to court and at all times were courteous when dealing with the family. DS Smith was aware that we as a family needed to know that they were working hard to bring a conviction. We were invited to the police station to meet with the investigating officers and witness the hard work for ourselves. We were informed that Police Officers were called back from days off and holidays to assist in the investigation. No stone was left unturned.

It personalised Dean and provided the family with hope that his would-be killers would be quickly detained and convicted. It provided us with the information that Dean was important and not just a victim. He was a son, husband, father, brother, grandson, uncle, nephew and friend.

On the day that I had to identify Dean, it was Faye and Adrian who drove us to the police mortuary. Whilst they did not enter the room they were by our side to support and guide us during the traumatic experience that we had to endure. They later assisted us when we had to call them regarding the media who were camped by our house as we arrived home from identifying Dean. We relied heavily upon the FLOs and I think it makes a difference to the family to have someone to depend upon and who they can trust.

I later remember talking to Faye and Adrian's boss Rhona who was trying to advocate for a support package for victims to be put in place. I informed her of our experience as the victim's family and what I thought would be helpful as part of a package. I guess we were lucky in that we were able to afford Dean's funeral, but other families were not so lucky. The government provide you with a £1,000 towards costs. Dean's funeral cost eight times that amount. Dean and Carol were a young couple with a young family so couldn't afford the costs. They struggled to make ends meet so did not have insurance policies. A number of families are in the same position but don't have relatives that could offer financial support. I believe the government should be providing more financial assistance.

Emotional support for families should be provided and prioritised by way of psychologists or counsellors immediately, and not six months down the line, after all the perpetrators have immediate access to counsellors, psychologists and social workers as do their families – who says crime doesn't pay. Practical support should be offered to families who are struggling to cope with things such as child care for families who want to attend court procedures or appointments.

I had asked Aberdeenshire Social Work department if they could help provide assistance with "holiday club" for the two older boys whilst the family were dealing with the police investigation. It would be too late to book places as they would already be filled. As a social worker I knew that social work would always have places for families in an emergency. Dean had been murdered during the Easter holidays so the children were not at school. Aberdeenshire Social Work department advised the family that they could not assist unless they opened a case, obviously we declined. It meant that the children were going to have to occupy themselves whilst the adults were busy answering questions, leaving three bewildered children.

As a family we also had to deal with the Housing department who were unhelpful initially due to one of the murderer's sister living next door to my other son's family. She had made threats towards his partner and the lady's children had made threats towards my grandchildren at school causing more grief. They eventually managed to re-house my family, but I had to seek assistance from local counsellors and the CEO of Housing before it occurred. Once again as a social worker I knew who to contact, other people may not know or have the strength to address these issues adding to their pain. A support package should be developed and when they hand you the book with information on how to deal with a murdered love one it should include all the supports that you can access as the victim's family. Sadly, I don't think the support package ever was developed. It is too late for my family but could prevent a lot of grief for other families.

So in reflection, if I could ever offer any advice to families experiencing the murder of a love one it is in your best interest to co-operate with the police and the FLOs. They will support and assist you as best that they can and provide the information that is necessary without jeopardising the case. As the family of a murdered victim you will experience many emotions and will sometimes be angry with the police if you feel nothing is happening, just remember they have to be extremely careful with information and evidence in order to build a case and get a conviction. The police are not the enemy, let them do their job and you will develop a good relationship with them and your Family Liaison Officers.

Information that I would tell the policy makers of the Justice system is that victims and victim's families need victims commissioners, they need to have the right to provide their victim impact statement in court in front of the jurors. They need to have the right to appeal the conviction and they need the right to be allowed to live without the fear of criminals appealing their conviction time after time. In my opinion the appeals should be capped at two. It destroys a family and hinders the grieving process to have to continually experience appeals. I personally believe that when someone receives a tariff of life then life should mean life.

Chapter 10

Media

From the beginning the media made our lives miserable. Trying to make sense of the evil that had entered our lives that day on the 4th of April 2006 and the loss of my son in such a horrific way, the family gathered together trying to figure out what had happened to Dean. Staring into space and trying to block out what we had been told, thinking this is a nightmare and I am stuck and cannot waken from it. *Please, won't somebody help me, make it better, let Dean walk into the room shouting, "You need to pay for my taxi mum," as he often did.* Only this was real. This was something that happened to other people, not to us.

They came in droves like hunters staking out their prey. They practically camped outside our door going from neighbour to neighbour. Banging on the door asking stupid questions such as 'how does the family feel?' My brother would answer the door but he was too nice, too diplomatic, until I answered the door screaming for them to leave us alone. I was incensed; could they not see the pain we were in and the intrusion that they were making into our lives? They were totally insensitive not taking no for an answer. "Go away," I would shout as my family looked on helplessly, not knowing what to do.

My poor mother, a broken woman who tried to comfort her daughter as best that she could, never normally lost for words. "Tell us about Dean," they cried. "How are his kids," some would say. They would always start off by saying, "I'm sorry to hear."

"No you're not," I cried, "you never knew him. He was not your child or family." It was like Dean became the property of the media. Every half hour they came barging in begging for a morsel of information that they could sensationalise. They would come right up to late evening. They would know what was happening before the police had told us. It was taking its toll on us until DS Smith advised us to co-operate with the media and that would give us back some control. He said we need the media to be on our side to catch these killers. They can put information out to the public that could help capture the people who had callously taken Dean's life. So I agreed to an interview with the BBC and Grampian television to plead for information.

As I faced the camera words failed me, dry mouthed and stuttering I tried to utter the words that had been provided by the police for any information that the public could provide. I sounded like a frightened cat with words barely audible. The presenter was very gentle and persuasive as he tried to put me at ease, encouraging me to continue as the tears coursed down my face. No sooner had the news been broadcast information came flooding in.

Research would suggest that in the last 30 or so years with the growth of 24-hour news channels, internet-only news sites and the decline of the newspaper, there have been tremendous changes in how the media covers crime. It is particularly important as most of the information that the public receives about crime come from the media and it is critical that the information be scrutinised and critiqued. According to the law all victims should be treated equally. It was my experience that victims are treated very differently.

The police were obviously aware of how the media operate and we as a family were advised to work with them and not against them as we needed to have the media on our side. At first I didn't get it but I have since found that it worked in our favour to work with them as the media coverage of crime victims often focus on personal, situational and demographic characteristics, which had nothing to do with the crime in itself. The media coverage affects the jury selection and decision making as well as the public sentiment. The police advised us not to antagonise the media as they were the key to finding out crucial information about Dean's murder. It would then surprise me that we heard vital information on the news about Dean's murder despite the police presence in our lives at the time.

Nevertheless, I hated how they would sensationalise the story, the more blood and guts they could manifest the better the readership, but the more traumatic for the family as they used descriptive words such as they 'butchered', him painting a really horrifying story for us the family to visualise the torture that Dean had to tolerate adding to our pain. Every time a story was reported on the news or in a newspaper we had to live and relive the suffering he had to endure. We found out in the newspaper that a man had filmed himself using a mobile phone jumping on Dean's head. A female witness described the footage like a horror movie as there was so much blood.

I died a death every time I read or heard the news being reported. It was big news in Scotland and I gather it went nationwide mainly because Dean was an innocent bystander and his only crime was that he was in the wrong place at the wrong time. The public was outraged and I guess Dean gained a lot of sympathy, but at what cost. His older children were affected badly as other children at school would comment on what they had heard their parents say - children can be cruel without meaning it. Another headline had suggested that they had cut off Dean's genitalia. Words could not describe what we as a family were going through. The police assured us that it was not true, but not before other children had told Dean's son. He was totally traumatised and we as a family were struggling to take the information in and poor Liam was going downhill fast. Words hold no meaning as you try and comfort a child who is beyond consoling. Why did the media have to be so graphic and embellish the truth, didn't they know the effect it was having on us, Dean's family, not to mention reliving the torture of a loved one that they had held so dear? We tried to shield the children as best we could, but to no avail.

We soon developed a relationship with the media, mostly the British Broadcasting Corporation and the Grampian Television news rooms who were very supportive of the family. Although, I have to say I was quite amused about how competitive they were in vying for the next interview. Colin Wight was the senior broadcaster of the BBC in Reporting Scotland and he was a gentleman in making you feel at ease and getting the best out of you. He always made sure that he was as sensitive as he could be when asking you questions, especially the difficult ones and then there was Gavin Robertson, or Robinson not sure which, who was the young, up and coming broadcaster who worked at Grampian Television. He was much more assertive in his interviewing and had a more direct way of questioning you, nevertheless he was also a gentleman.

I guess the thing that would upset the family the most is how they stalked you during the trial when they practically chased you up the street as you entered the court and the same as you left. We eventually got used to it. There were quite a number of newspaper reporters in the court, and as you entered you felt their eyes upon you watching your expression, what you wore and who was with you. You got to know who was okay and who was not, who could understand at the end of the day that you were exhausted listening to the horror story unwind in court on your loved one's last few hours of life as he was brutally murdered.

It was fair to say that the police were right. You have to work with the media and I have found in doing so they would leave you alone as best they could. At the end of the trial we had to attend a press conference and DS Smith asked if myself and Dean's wife Carol would accompany him and we could get the interviews over, with all the press present at the one time. We agreed to do so and as a family we prepared a statement that I would read out before they had the opportunity to ask any questions. Detective Superintendent Alan Smith who led the murder investigation said, "Dean was the victim of an incredibly senseless killing. Chosen at random, that poor man was subjected to a frenzied, relentless attack, akin that to a pack mentality, which was as humiliating and degrading as it was violent."

I was next and was shaking in my shoes. I was unsure whether I could do this and was scared stiff. The light was scorching my eyes and I could not see a thing which I guess was lucky for me. I asked Dean to help me get through the interview and a certain calm came over me. I read the statement that we as a family prepared.

"Today's verdict, whilst welcomed by the family, in no way compensates for the pain and heartache experienced by the family since Dean's death. In particular, it cannot and does not compensate for the loss of a father, a son and a husband who was adored by his family and who was killed for being in the wrong place at the wrong time. The murderers of Dean, convicted today, are despicable individuals, devoid of conscience, who share equal responsibility for his death regardless of tariff. In seeking to endure Dean's death and the circumstances that surround it we are bound together by an absolute belief that his death ends nothing; that in death as in life he continues to guide, console and support those he holds dear and that his death only ends that part of our relationship that was physical. For you see you can't kill a memory, a whispered endearment, a stolen hug or a love so intense that it surmounts and eclipses the most grave of circumstances.

In closing we would ask that the media to respect our right to continue our healing process, devoid of their intervention and we would thank those who have supported us throughout, in particular Detective Chief Superintendent Alan Smith and his team at Grampian police for their rigorous and exhaustive preparation of the evidence, pertaining to the case and the family would also like to wish to express its tremendous appreciation to Fay Tough and Adrian Brewster of the Grampian Police Family Liaison, for the support given throughout the judicial process. It brought great comfort and eased our stress. We would finally thank the press and media for conducting themselves in a professional manner with little intrusion into the family's life and we would ask that they continue in this exemplary conduct and allow the family to grieve privately."

The questions by the media then came fast and furious to us. Carol, Dean's wife, was beyond despair and fled crying and it was then left to DS Alan Smith and I to continue. I am unsure where I got the strength to get through the press conference, but I do feel I got a little help from divine intervention.

I presume what was most upsetting was the magazines who wanted to sensationalise Dean's story. I didn't want to be sitting in some doctors or dentist room reading a magazine and Dean come popping up. They came in every shape and form and they always said the same thing, they wanted to pay tribute to Dean and how sorry they were. I guess it is their job to find stories for their magazine but it was not the right time. They offered money and I suppose Dean's family could have done with it especially leading up to Christmas, but we as a family, especially Dean's wife, discussed whether we were willing to put his story in a magazine and we all agreed that we couldn't, at least not at that time. We have all read the hard luck stories and the horror stories in magazines and we didn't want Dean's to be one of them.

It was bad enough that it was spread across the news and on television, but it was out of our control and it was intrusive. Perhaps that is why I am writing this book. I am in control and it is my story, not some magazine or newspaper. I initially was going to use a ghost writer but then it became their story of events with my input but it was how they wanted to write the book. I didn't feel I had the skills as I knew nothing about writing but was persuaded to give it a try. I suppose in reflection and since, the media has been kind to my family and have supported me in every way possible when I have campaigned for certain events, such as the closure of the Forensic Department in Aberdeen. If I have to say anything to the media, it is to be mindful to the family and sensitive in their line of questioning and to remember that what they write has an impact on the family for the rest of their lives, especially if there are children involved.

Chapter 11

Last Touch

The moment had finally arrived, Dean had to be identified, he was my child I had brought him into the world now I would have to see him out. Fear gripped me, how could I bear it. It felt like a vice was twisting my heart. What would I see? Inside I was screaming and dying, at the same time on the outside I had the stiff upper lip and was in control. Gareth, my son, Carol, Deans wife, and my friend Elaine accompanied me. I didn't have the energy to tell Elaine I didn't want her there but she came anyway, it's funny how even words become a heavy burden. The police liaison officers drove us to the police mortuary a journey that felt like hours but had only taken twenty minutes.

Gazing out of the window I saw police men searching through the countryside, it hadn't dawned on me that they were searching for Dean's clothes. We drove in deathly silence to our destination where we were met by

Dr James Grieve and his assistant, the criminal pathologist. I knew James Grieve during my days as a student radiographer when I attended his lectures and had observed him undertaken a post mortem on a murder victim who had been killed by a taxi driver. How ironic it seems now. It had taken place in the police mortuary and I remember being horrified to see him eating sandwiches beside the body. I asked him how he could eat his sandwiches on site and he said that he had to detach himself or he couldn't do his job. This was just another job for him, but this was my son.

I stood there, fear gripping me, wanting to run like a frightened rabbit. They slowly drew back the curtains and behind the glass wall lay my beautiful baby son with his elfin shaped face, his hair in curls, oh how he would have hated that, he went to great lengths to keep it straight. His navy blue eyes were devoid of life. Oh, how I ached to gather him in my arms and tell him he was going to be alright. Only I wasn't allowed to touch him for fear of tainting the evidence. The shock was too much and I hit the deck like a stone, immediately getting back up. I could not breathe as the realisation that my son was gone, dead hit me like a bolt of lightning, just one last touch was all I wanted. It had a double dichotomy meaning as when Dean and my daughter Kerrie were growing up they had a little game they would play as they left the house where they would pot each other run out and say, "Last touch." This continued throughout childhood and became their ritual in adulthood.

The journey home was harrowing, reality finally sinking in, not a word passed anyone's mouth. A family traumatised, not good at voicing how they feel, stiff upper lip and all that. Terror, fear, gripped my very soul, there was no mistaking, Dean was gone and in his place was a shell. No more silly phone calls, no more annoying late night calls asking for a lift, no more pranks, no more singing and no more Dean. I couldn't think, I didn't want to think, the pain was too raw – what happens next and what do I do? I'm afraid this is no dress rehearsal, no script is provided. I couldn't bear to leave Dean on that cold hard slab, all alone. He wouldn't want to be on his own, but you have no voice, no choice and you have no control, he no longer belongs to you, he is the property of a criminal investigation.

As we approached home I noticed the media looming in the background, how do we escape the car without being seen? I wanted to scream obscenities at them, how dare they invade our space at such a devastating time, had they no shame? We rushed into the house trying to avoid any contact with them, to the sound of them calling for a few minutes of our time.

"How's the family feeling Mrs Jamieson?"

I wanted to call back, "How the fuck do you think we are feeling?" Instead I said, "No comment."

A deathly silenced hit me as we entered the house, all eyes on us as the family waited for information on what took place at the police mortuary. A sense of weariness washed over me as I tried to find the words to tell the family that their brother, dad, grandson and nephew was really gone and not coming back. His children unusually quiet and well-behaved, not knowing what was happening, only that it was something bad as the adults were going around with sad and tear stained faces. "Where is dad?" his youngest child would say, not understanding that he would not be coming home, not now not ever. He was 3 years old and already without a father, his buddy. Who would sit him on his lap at bedtime and give him his 'coozzie boozzie', a special ritual that the two of them shared. Dean was one for rituals.

My heart went out to them, so young and already having to experience great pain in life, only it was to get worse. It was a sad day in the Jamieson residence as family and friends came to grips with the awful reality of what had just occurred, the sense of finality, where no hope was to be had. The house was busy with other family and friends dropping by to offer their condolences, food and flowers dropped off, meals were made, it was a hive of activity, with not a metre that you could call your own space. I wanted to seek refuge in my room to lick my wounds, but even that wasn't free, so people sat around like zombies unable to function in a normal manner, getting on with their daily business. There was no escaping, every news channel every newspaper was blasting, "Young Kemnay dad of four Dean Jamieson murdered and left to die on Elrick Hill next to Craibstone golf club."

Dean became a headline, "the victim." I am sure each time a newsreader said, "Murdered father of four," no one flinched except us, his family. The media took his life and kneaded it into tabloid fodder and in doing so almost took his identity and his memory. We were listening to the newscaster night after night with distain as he used an appropriately bold and sombre tone to announce the sensational slaying. It was close to home, so it was big news. To the newscaster it was just the lead story on a great night of news, sure to rate well. His baritone seemed almost callous as he depersonalised Dean once again for the public viewing and told them the gory details of what they all wanted to hear. I remember thinking *well, you've got your dream Dean, you always wanted to be famous* only I don't quite think it would have been quite in the horrific circumstances that were unfolding.

News was coming in fast and furious. Mostly we would hear through the media before the police provided the information, it wasn't that they withheld the information they were simply being cautious. We understood that. It was important that they caught the perpetrator, or perpetrators, for at that point we were in the dark. Day after day the FLOs would appear and day after day the questions would hurl. We could hardly take anymore. The media were forever at our door and the same answer would be provided, "No comment," you would think that they would give up until finally the police advised us to co-operate with them.

A press conference was to occur and the family asked to appeal for witnesses. So keeping in order with what the police requested we paid tribute to Dean in hope that the profile would help identify his killers. Dean was a committed family man above anything else, who loved his wife and children dearly. He was also a social, affable individual who embraced life in its many forms. We remembered Dean as a scoundrel, a poet, a philosopher and as a lay historian who had a thirst for knowledge and self education. He was also a son, a brother, a father, a husband, a grandson, a nephew and a friend and in each role he enriched the lives of those he held dear. It was hoped that the tribute would allow the public to see Dean as your normal 'Joe Bloggs', warts and all and to provide any information to the police that could lead to the arrest of Deans killer.

The next day - the 8th April - a breakthrough occurred and four Aberdeen men were arrested with his murder. On 10th April Colin Cowie, 21, Colin Stewart, also 21, Kevin Leslie, 23, and Shaun Paton, 20, appeared in private at Aberdeen Sherriff Court. The men, all from Aberdeen, made no plea or declaration and were remanded in custody for further examination. When we heard the news we were relieved that his killers were off the streets and hoped that justice would prevail. Our next door neighbour was a policeman and had to be taken off his normal duties as the four individuals were locked up in the cells where he worked. We had lived next door for the past 12 years and he had watched Dean grow up. We were pretty close as neighbours go, so it was not a good idea for him to be working in close proximity with the four killers.

Dc Alan Smith later advised that it was the killer's own community that had led to the four men being charged and convicted of Dean's murder. He said that it was Shaun Paton, Kevin Leslie and Colin Cowie's own "arrogance and cockiness" in bragging to those on the estate that ensured they did not get away with their "cowardly attack". Alan Smith stated that he thought one of the downfalls of all those involved was their arrogance and assuredness that, in speaking to those in the community – family and friends – they would not be betrayed. They couldn't have got that more wrong. He said that through the media, there was a high level of calls to the control room. A number of those in the community had been totally disgusted by what they had done and were willing to engage with the enquiry team and were willing to give specific evidence which had led to the recovery of items of clothes that Dean had been wearing on the night he was killed.

Dean's older son at this point was starting to suffer; he could read the newspapers and was quite distressed by what they were saying. Nothing could console him, why did someone hurt his dad he would say and we couldn't find an answer. Friends from school would say things to him from what they had overheard their parents say and kids could be cruel until one day he punched one of the kids out of sheer frustration. It was totally out of character and not acceptable. The final straw was when we found him behind the settee hitting his head off the ground, we were concerned for him, he was crying out for help. When a violent death occurs you are handed a booklet about how to cope with the death of a loved one and as a family we were not emotionally equipped to provide the support and help that a young child requires as we are too involved with our own grief. So I contacted victim support and asked them what support they could provide, none was the honest answer.

As a social worker I fix things for a living so I contacted the Children's Counselling Services and asked for an appointment for my grandchildren who were currently experiencing trauma as the consequence of their father's brutal murder only to be told that there was a six month waiting list. It beggared belief. Dean's children wandered in a haze of pain and confusion, his killers were coddled and cooed over lest the system did them any damage. Do not damage the damaged. Four young men killed a man so therefore they must be broken and must be put back together again by the system with access to psychologists, counsellors and social workers on tap, such is the prison regime. Dean's children had access to a six-month waiting list. Where is the fairness in that? Surely we live in a democracy that states that justice is rooted in fairness, obviously not. Using my professional prowess I managed to access counselling in a shorter time scale but it took up a lot of time and energy that I just didn't possess.

The days that followed became a blur, I remember going to the bank and for no reason just burst out crying, it would hit you at any time. There were to be several similar episodes like that in the days that followed. My life was in shreds, the person I was would be no more, darkness became my world for a long period. My friend the medium came to the house one day and said that she had information that she needed to pass onto the police. I was unsure whether they would be up for it or not, as not everyone believes in the afterlife or that mediums speak to the dead. The two FLOs agreed to listen to what she had to say and I remember she drew a picture of a man that she thought was the ring leader and it wasn't until the men were identified that we realised that it was a dead ringer for Kevin Leslie, she also advised that there were four men involved in the murder and that they had taken him to a secluded area where they had dropped him off, and that they would find some of his clothes in one of the young men's attic, there were other things that she said only I cannot remember. At this point pictures of the men had not been released and that it wasn't until the trial that we found out that they had initially put Dean's clothes in the attic before they tried to get rid of them. I don't know what the police done with the information, if they took note or not. I only know that some things were pretty accurate, some not.

It gave me comfort to know that Dean was trying to communicate from the afterlife and that he was looking down on his family. Whether people believe or not it's up to the individual and you do what you can to survive the death of your loved one; some attend counselling, some contact support groups and some contact psychics in the hope they have a message from their dearly departed. I chose the latter.

I needed my child home, I begged for his return but they couldn't release his body as the Crown had to undertake a post mortem on Dean as well as all four defence lawyers. It tore at my very heart to have these strangers hack into my son's broken body and I agonised over every cut as I imagined the mutilation that was occurring and was worried about how I would eventually find him when he returned home. It also pained me that they put him into a cold, dark refrigerator like a piece of meat every night all alone. So I waited, until eventually I was told that he could come home and then I was hit with another clanger, he would be minus his brain. I had an option I could wait and bury him now or I would have to wait until after the trial in case they needed further evidence. Murder victims cannot be cremated, they have to be buried in case further evidence is required and their body has to be exhumed. I chose to have Dean home as soon as possible so that he could be laid to rest and his family spend time with him. This would take three weeks.

Chapter 12

Final Journey Home

Dean's greatest fear was being left on his own and it was three weeks before he finally made that journey home. He was taken to Berridale Funeral Parlour in Westhill, Aberdeen where he would be made ready for burial. I wanted the coffin lid off so I could see and touch him but they advised against it. He had had to endure three post mortems they said, but I needed to touch him. Along with my daughter Kerrie and Carol his wife we made our way to the parlour where they had placed Dean in his coffin ready to view. Both Carol and Kerrie ran from the room crying saying it wasn't Dean but it was, he was my baby.

We had taken some of his personal items, photos and letters from his children and I cut off a lock of his hair as a keepsake. I sat and spoke to him for a while and told him justice would be done and that I would make sure his children would be alright. I leaned over and kissed his ice-cold face and finally had my last touch. I felt his presence as I said my final goodbye before they closed the lid. I was a broken woman, my baby callously ripped from this world just for being in the wrong place at the wrong time.

It was a crisp cold afternoon when Dean finally arrived at the home where he had grown up. I stood at the window waiting for him. I had prepared a spot in the house where he would lie in his Anderson Tartan Coffin. If you knew Dean then you would know that he liked the best and the best he was going to have. There he lay for the next three days and I never left his side until he was to be buried.

It was a sad, sad day when Dean was brought home, his children perplexed as they couldn't understand what was happening. His youngest kept asking what was in the box and we replied 'your dad' and he asked if he was hiding. We struggled to tell him the truth as he was too young to understand. People came to pay their last respects and once again the house was like Glasgow Sauchiehall Street you couldn't move. I was desperate for the family to spend some time with Dean, to speak about the good and the bad times, but that was not to be. Dean had now become public domain.

The day before Dean was to be buried we wanted to have a small service for his children, something that was important for them. It was their time to speak about their dad and say a final goodbye as the adults the next day would be overcome with grief and the children forgotten. We bought some helium balloons and the children wrote their special message and the minister said a prayer, the children on a dark cold night let off their balloons into the sky. Neil, our neighbour, noticed that the balloons were all heading towards Craibstone Golf Course where Dean was found, it was quite surreal.

Family had arrived from Ayrshire and there was not a seat or space in the house that you could sit on. As per our custom a 'wake' is held and family stay up most of the night with a drink in hand speaking to the deceased about their life. I'm pretty sure Dean was present as he would have wanted to hear what everyone was saying and join in with the camaraderie, it was a celebration of his life where everyone told their special story and there was much laughter as they remembered Dean with great fondness.

At last everyone went to bed and Dean and I were alone together, at first I could not speak, I had so much I wanted to say but was unable to utter the words, I eventually whispered to him, afraid that I might wake him up, about the day he was born and how I was the happiest person alive and what joy he had brought me, I spoke about his first faltering steps and how I was there to catch him. I spoke about his first day at nursery when he refused to let me go and how I was there to hold his hand and wipe his tears. I spoke about his first day at school when all I could do was cry as I watched him entering the classroom now a big boy who didn't need his mum so much, as he turned around and smiled as he waved me off. I spoke about the times when he was an adolescent and the trials and tribulations that he brought me and how I was there to guide and support him and the painful journey that it sometimes was, when at times he drove me to distraction. I spoke of his first love and the devastation that he went through when it ended and how I held him in my arms as he wept bitterly. I spoke about the birth of his first child when we embraced with tears of love as he gazed into her beautiful face. I spoke of the birth of his three boys when he said that with every child his love for them grew and grew. I spoke about his wedding when I saw that happy but nervous groom and how proud of him I was. I spoke about his death and the pain I felt at not being there to protect and save him from evil and mostly I spoke about how much I, we, as a family would miss him and the devastation that we all felt and life that we knew would be no more and I cried and I cried like no tomorrow, my life in ruins.

The day that I was about to bury my son had finally arrived and I was unsure that I would be able to take this journey. Family were still arriving from Ayrshire and now people were waiting outside in the garden, the nearest and dearest, if only Dean knew how loved and important he was in people's lives. The police piper arrived and the music was chosen, I'm not sure what was eventually played only that it touched our deepest emotions, the haunting voice of the bagpipes expressed the feelings that words alone fail to convey. The men were all dressed in the Anderson Tartan and I wanted his final journey to be full of pomp and importance as Dean was in life. The time had arrived and the undertakers were at the door to take Dean to his final resting place.

We had chosen a plot in the picturesque village of Skene next to where a few young people lay as it was important that he was not on his own next to the elderly. Silly I know. The media had requested to film his funeral but I felt that it was too intrusive and I did not want the world to witness the pain we felt as we finally laid Dean to rest. I compromised and allowed the service to be taped for wireless. I asked the reporters not to be too close to the funeral party and to give us our dignity. I was crushed as I watched my husband, brothers, sons and friend carry my beloved son following the hearse and the piper out of the street where he had grown up, his two young sons following closely behind, his final journey.

Family and friends filled the Skene Parish church to pay tribute to Dean and as mourners entered the church, we played *Angels* by Robbie Williams, a song that he often sang to me after a couple of drinks. This song will always have a special place in my heart and to this day when I hear it, it brings a tear to my eye as it brings back memories and how he is no longer with us. The Reverend Iain Thompson held the service; he had known Dean as a child when he attended Sunday school and Scouts he said that he was a "much loved, well liked mischievous man," who was cared deeply for by his family. We chose the hymns *O Lord my God, When I in Awesome Wonder* and *Morning has Broken*, hymns that were fitting to Dean. A family friend who knew Dean as a child spoke on our behalf and delivered his Eulogy, at that point I felt my whole world had ended. I struggled to remain in control when all I wanted to do was scream and shout I wanted my baby back. No mother should ever have to bury their child. I pleaded with God to end my nightmare but I knew it would never end.

We left the church to enter the graveyard to James Blunt *Goodbye My Lover,* chosen by his wife Carol, I was later informed that there was not a dry eye in the church. By this time I could hardly place one foot in front of the other. The piper escorted us to Dean's final resting place as he played a lament, its haunting music causing an eerie silence to occur as people held their own memories and thoughts of Dean. It had been a cold drizzly day and I hoped that it would remain dry and as we laid him to rest, a rainbow appeared and a white dove flew over, I somehow think that Dean was in the procession watching his own funeral and making sure I had got it right.

We walked the few yards to the bar where we held a tea, there we met some of Dean's schoolboy friends who informed me that they were Dean's real friends, not the ones that he had recently been associating with. His old Drama teacher was present and upset looking, old beyond his years. Friends who I hadn't seen for years were there paying their last respects. A new child was born into the family that day, we sure wouldn't miss that birthday. I ached to leave but had to remain to greet the mourners, smile stuck on my face thanking those that attended.

My grandson Liam, Dean's oldest son came up to me and asked if I felt any better, knowing that it was important to him so that he would feel better, I said, "A little bit."

He said to me, "I look like my dad don't I?"

I replied, "Yes you do."

Liam said, "One day I'll have children and they'll look like me, then dad will never die."

Out the mouth of babes, a wise young boy only eight years old, who had his dad cruelly snatched away. I did feel a little bit better, Liam had put a smile on my face; how very true his words were. As I often think of his words I look at all four children who resemble Dean in many ways and a look or glance reminds me that Dean will never truly die as his children are testaments of him.

On the way home the men stopped at a couple of bars and toasted Dean. They had a collage made up of Dean growing up and it had pride of place on every bar, he would have loved that as he loved going out with his brothers, father, uncles and friends, not that he done it often as Dean was mostly a lone drinker. They then came home and everyone sat around telling stories about Dean. There was some laughter at his antics as Dean was always the clown, mimicking people and making us laugh and there were lots of tears. The drink loosening people's emotions, that stiff upper lip gone and people being true to themselves. No bed again that night, two and three to a bed. I cried out for solitude, for space to grieve the loss of my precious son. Gareth told us the next day that he had a dream that Dean had come to him and that he had looked up to the ceiling and Dean was there dancing in what would have been his wedding clothes smiling down at him. He said he was freaked out as it was so real. Maybe Dean did come to let Gareth know that all was well and that he was fine. I would like to think that.

Morning has broken and along with that, people were packing and returning to their own homes and lives and all of a sudden the house was quiet. The last casserole dish is picked up and the outside world stops grieving with you. The children were back at school and all that was left was Kerrie and Gareth who both had returned to work. Gordon, my husband, decided to have a golfing holiday before returning to work in New Zealand and I didn't know what to do. Time isn't a good thing for people experiencing a tragic death. I would go over the chain of events until I made myself ill. At least when the house was full I was busy and did not have time to think – isn't this what I wanted, space and freedom to reflect, think and make sense of all that had occurred?

Sleep evaded me. I got upset one day when it rained as I worried that Dean would get cold with no protection from the elements. I didn't make sense. I would go to the shops and forget what I had gone for. People evaded you, they were afraid to speak as they didn't know what to say. I was drowning and there was no way out. So I returned to work, I thought it best to get back to normal as quick as I could and I seemed to function largely as before. The mask that I wore for the world was carefully constructed and effective. I seemed to epitomise what many people would call 'doing really well', meaning someone who had experienced a loss but looked as if I was finished grieving. The truth of my life was something else. I remained in deep despair, exhausted from acting better than I felt around co-workers, family and friends.

My employer Aberdeen City Council in their youthful wisdom had moved me to another department as my Team Leader was also my friend and neighbour and had experienced the whole tragic event alongside me.She didn't think that she would be able to cope with me in her team as it would be too stressful, so they moved me to another team where I didn't know very many people and I felt isolated. Another loss and change, I didn't have my usual colleagues around to support me when I felt myself spiralling out of control. The first day back was a nightmare, people avoided me and I could see the quick glances and the whispering within the office as people looked my way. I sat at my desk unable to move, paralysed with fear wondering if I would ever feel normal again. I ran to the toilets and sobbed afraid someone might hear. Would the pain ever cease?

The pain never leaves you, but it lessens and you eventually cope with the loss of your child. It is your pain and your child is at peace, no more pain or heartache for them, so you are left grieving for yourself. One day you wake up and there is brightness in the sky, you laugh at your friend's jokes and you go dancing. Suddenly you are alive again. Embrace life as it's precious.

Chapter 13

The Trial

Monday 16th October 2006

Today is the day when the trial officially begins and as a family we are bracing ourselves. It is cold and the sky is grey and we wonder if there is snow in the air as we leave the house to hear the housekeeping news before the trial gets on the way. We are dreading having to be in the same room as Dean's killers as we know we will come face to face with them. The jury is picked and a lot of them appear to be quite young and I don't know if this is a good thing.

Colin Cowie has offered the court a plea of guilty to culpable homicide but thankfully the Crown has refused it. Adrian Cottam has gone up in my estimation. The preliminaries are out of the way and the questioning will begin the next day. I had met Depute Advocate Adrian Cottam during preliminaries in Edinburgh prior to the trial beginning. I had no faith in him due to an earlier preliminary hearing when he appeared ill-prepared and took a barraging from the Judge. I'm afraid I told Adrian Cottam that I had no faith in his ability to act on the Crown's behalf. This boy, because that is how I saw him initially, assured me that he would make sure that he would work as hard as he could to secure convictions. He initially didn't want to meet me. By the end of the trial this boy became a man and I have nothing but admiration for him. He was a fresh-faced young man at the start but by the end he was completely exhausted. He kept his word.

Tuesday 17th October 2006

Fingernails chewed to the quick, heart racing, I have waited patiently for this hour and day to appear. Justice has to prevail, these four evil men will be going behind bars for a long time that I was sure. It was a cold brisk morning as we set off as a family to attend the first day of the trial of the four accused of murdering my son. As we got near to the High court in Aberdeen we saw the media van parked at the side of the road. I felt the rage rise within me as they ran towards us filming as we entered the courtroom. It felt like we were being violated as if the camera had access to my very soul.

I scanned the room to see a familiar face and right enough there stood both Liaison Officers. We had developed a close relationship with these two people who had delivered the worse news possible. They became a great support to us and I don't think we could have managed the trial without these two guys protecting, supporting and providing us with information. As we entered the courtroom we were informed that there was a suspected gas leak in the street and we had to vacate the building.

It was reconvened only to be disrupted again after a DVD player broke down. It was to be used to show the jurors video footage of Elrick Hill where Dean was found. Evidence was instead given by meteorologist Richard Tabony who worked at the Met Office. He read a report that told the jurors that weather readings taken at Aberdeen Airport had been close to freezing and where Dean was found was at least one per cent higher and colder, it was also snowing.

We found ourselves sitting directly behind the four accused of murdering Dean: Shaun Paton, Kevin Leslie, Colin Stewart and Colin Cowie. Four normal-looking young men. I kept on looking for signs that showed them to be murderers, there was none. What had happened in their lives to turn them into sociopaths with no remorse or feelings for robbing an innocent young man who they didn't know of his life in such a horrific manner. Crazy thoughts were running through my mind, I wanted to pulverise them for what they did to my child, to squeeze the very life out of them, but that would make me no better than them. I abhor violence, even the slaying of a spider, but these vermin I so wanted to beat them to a pulp until they screamed for mercy for the sadistic torture they had inflicted upon my son Dean.

We no longer had a son, my children no longer a brother, his children no longer a father, his wife no longer a husband, grandparents had lost a grandson and so on. Our family was devastated, words cannot tell how we were feeling, the depths of despair that we had reached. I wanted revenge and hatred filled my very soul, something that was alien to me now became my friend, my dark passenger.

We knew that Dean had been stripped at knifepoint, slashed with knives, beaten and left to die in temperatures below freezing. The four men accused Kevin Leslie, Colin Stewart, Colin Cowie and Shaun Paton had taken Dean in what he thought was a taxi to an isolated golf course called Craibstone at Elrick Hill Aberdeen. All four men denied murder and kidnap. A hushed silence spread over the court as the words were uttered. Thank God I was sitting as it hit me like a bolt of lightning. I thought I was prepared for what I was about to hear about how they had killed Dean, but all I wanted to do was run. Run as far away as possible but I couldn't, I was rooted to the chair paralysed by fear for what they may say next.

Mr Eddie, Cowie's cousin, was the next witness and he was terrified as he gave evidence as he was told that if he said anything in court he would end up the same way as Dean. He was a reluctant witness and at one point left the court knocking over a chair saying he was leaving. He was persuaded to come back but he kept on saying he was scared and that he didn't want to testify. He was initially in the car when they picked Dean up but was taken back to Aunty Mary Stotts to allow Shaun Paton to take his place. He suspected something was going to happen but didn't want to be involved. He said Cowie told him everything when he got back and asked him to help clean blood off his trainers. They went up a country road and threw the trainers out the car. Mr Eddie said that Cowie used the car as an unregistered taxi on numerous occasions. Cowie also showed him a video on the phone of Dean being beaten but Eddie said he couldn't look as he was sickened. Bastards, bastards, bastards.

Wednesday 18th October 2006

Today's first witness was Thomas McDonald, a cleaner who had been living in a caravan and had parked at the foot of the hill where Dean had been found. He said that he had gone to bed at 9.30 p.m. but had been woken some time later by headlights and a car engine driving into the car park and driving back out again. He said that he had left the area as it had been snowing and he didn't want to be snowed in. I sometimes wonder if Mr McDonald had been more observant would Dean still be alive?

Mr Edgar was the next witness, he is Shaun Paton's best friend. He had a very short and shoddy memory and couldn't remember anything. However, after the Depute Advocate read out his statement he remarkably got his memory back. He put all four accused at the scene of the crime. He said that on Paton's return he had blood stained trainers in his hands as well as a bloody knife. He also said that he heard Paton and Leslie go into the bathroom and wash the knife clean. He said that Paton had swapped trainers as he had been wearing Dean's trainers. The boy said he had put the trainers up into the loft. Paton shouted "Shite" at one point and Mr Edgar turned the story around. First time he said that both him and Paton put the trainers up in the loft then he said that it was only him. Colin Cowie's QC Dungood put it to Edgar that he was trying to protect Paton. Edgar replied that he was.

Thursday 19th October 2006

The day continued with both Edgar and Eddie's statements, where they advised that they had witnessed the boys coming back from murdering Dean and they had told him that they had just battered someone and had given him Dean's trainers.

Next witness was Joanne Cameron taking the stand. Right from the beginning she was defiant, abusive and swore at Her Ladyship and Depute Advocate She was given many warnings and spoken to by Her Ladyship. She constantly swore and had attitude. The audience was stunned, the clerk's mouth was agape, however she continued to behave badly with members of the judiciary trying to persuade her to cooperate. After many stops and starts the trial had to be abandoned. This was a sixteen year old girl who was terrified from the accused and did not know how to behave as she was afraid to give evidence in front of them. I almost felt sorry for her.

Joanne Cameron was asked to go into the witness box to continue with her evidence. This she refused to do. The case was adjourned to allow some negotiation to occur with various options and choices to get Joanne into the box. She still continued to refuse. Her Ladyship had no choice but to charge Joanne with contempt of court and put her in prison until the trial ends.

Next witness was Shaun Paton's brother who was sixteen. He was very nervous but I believe to be as truthful as he could. He placed all four boys at the scene of the crime and said that he had watched his brother try to conceal a bag of articles at a bookmakers in the Cumming Park Civil. He also said that he saw his brother with a knife and blood on his trainers. The defences tried to discredit him and his brothers. QC Mhairi Richards put it to him that he was the one who tried to conceal the articles but he managed to refute that. I was aware how difficult it must have been for him to stand against his brother.

Next witness was Shaun Paton's mother who took the stand. She told the truth selectively, it was obvious that she was minimising the statement and played on the fact that she had terminal cancer although in remission at present. She also played to the sympathy vote on Shaun Paton having ADHD. The defence was gentle with her.

A debate then took place regarding the next witness who was to be a policeman who would read out Joanne's statement. However the defence objected to this and a debate was heard and the court adjourned until Monday.

Monday 23rd October 2006

Let the circus begin.

Today was quite harrowing. My confidence has grown with the judge as she allowed Section 259, this permits an accused to use evidence from their co-accused's police interview, to go ahead and to reject the defence who wanted to give Joanne Cameron another chance. Her Ladyship had already said that prosecution could go for a Section 259 as it met the criteria. Joanne Cameron has refused to enter the witness box. I had been confident that she would and I was glad. The policeman read out Joanne's statement which was awful. She put all of the boys at the place of the scene and said they all took part in the crime. The story was consistent with the other witnesses and all said the same thing. The defence tried to discredit the police by saying that he had written the statement in his own words. He refuted that statement.

Next witness was Samantha Stott - the cousin of Colin Cowie. She was very upset and nervous at the prospect of having to give evidence and decided she couldn't remember anything. However, Adrian Cottam, Depute Advocate, put her statement to her and she agreed that she was telling the truth.

This was quite distressing as she was very graphic. Once again it put all four of the accused at the place of the scene and was consistent with the rest of the witnesses. Samantha cried throughout. The defence were quite gentle but totally confused her. QC Dungood,

Colin Stewart's barrister, told her she was lying and that he was totally innocent.

It was like a scene from a movie as the defence acted like bullies and lied throughout the questioning. Colin Stewart was acquitted of murder and just before the tape was put on with Colin Stewart exonerating himself from any part in the crime. He said that it was Shaun Paton and Colin Cowie who had murdered Dean and that he had tried to prevent it. He said he saw a knife but didn't see it being used. His memory was selective and he didn't place Kevin Leslie at the scene.

Chatting afterwards to Adrian Brewster he said that he hadn't expected the prosecution to pull the red herring so quickly, especially after seeing Shaun Paton's reaction who became extremely angry and agitated. Colin Cowie's face showed no emotion and as time goes on Colin Stewart's head is buried. Kevin Leslie is still a bit cocky.

Tuesday 24th October 2006

Today was quite a waste. One member of the jury is sick. The case is adjourned until this afternoon. Before that we have been informed by John Richardson Procurator Fiscal that Colin Stewart will be taking the witness stand. At first I was angry, however throughout the trial no one has pointed the finger at him. And although he was present he did try to stop it. Albeit he didn't phone an ambulance or the police. John said it was about using what you could to get a conviction, he also believed that Colin Stewart would not have been accused of murder and it was felt he would make a good witness. Although I believe this, I did it reluctantly.

It would appear in this case that there has been a lot of incidents which have held the case up and I will be glad when it finishes. I find that I hate the phone in the evening as I don't want to speak about court proceedings at night. It is bad enough to listen to the brutal slaying of Dean during the day. But the day will come if Stewart is let off then he will have to watch his back from the families and friends of the other three men left in the dock.

A debate then got into about the next witness who was to be a policeman who would read out Joanne's statement. However, the defence objected to this and a debate was heard and the court adjourned until Monday.

Wednesday 25th October 2006

Today we were only in court for a few moments. Colin Stewart was released and he will enter the witness box tomorrow to give evidence against the other three for the price of his freedom.

Gas man going to fix Kerrie's roof today; for some reason it is an exceptionally bad day. I have got a sore neck from concentrating at court but I am missing Dean like crazy and the movie is starting to become a reality. I need to hear his voice and touch him. The pain is unbearable and at times it feels like my heart is about to burst out my chest. I need a sign from him to let me know he is here.

Thursday 26th October 2006

Colin Stewart stepped into the witness box after noon to begin giving evidence against the three remaining accused. Stewart told the court that Dean had flagged down what he thought was a taxi and gave his name as "Deano." He described him as a young man who was out enjoying himself. He said that Dean got in the front of the car and asked Cowie to take him to Kemnay for £30.00. He said that during the journey a conversation was conducted in a language known in Northfield as "Eggy", Cowie later picked up Paton and he said that during the conversation they had planned to take Dean home and then wait until he was inside his house before sneaking back in to steal his belongings if his fare had not been paid.

Friday 27th October 2006

Stewart was today continuing to provide evidence against his three former friends. He told of how Dean had tried to escape half naked from his attackers. He claimed that one of the accuser's trousers had been "drenched in blood" after they had left Dean to die at Elrick Hill. Stewart said that during the journey they had went to a petrol station and Cowie had asked Dean for money to pay for the petrol and he refused saying that he would get the money when he got home to Kemnay.

Stewart informed the court that they then drove to Elrick Hill and dragged Dean out of the car and told him to take off his jumper and T shirt and then punched him in the face. He said that Dean ran away and bumped into Kevin Leslie who had punched him in the head with a knife in his hand. Dean had run down in the hill towards a car park and a camper van but had fallen on the way. Cowie then started fighting Dean. Stewart said that Paton kicked him a few times. Stewart denied that they had tried to cut off Dean's private parts. He claimed that after he had returned home he had tried to get Cowie to take him back to where they had left Dean but Cowie had allegedly said that he had been and Dean was no longer there.

Monday 30th October 2006

A witness called Miss Lynch had told the court that she overhead Kevin Lesley talking about what he had done to Dean. He said that he wanted to take a fillet out of his side as a keepsake. He then demonstrated on Miss Lynch's leg a sawing action. She said that he had told her that he had stabbed him on his cheek. Miss Lynch had told the court that Lesley had tried to scrape off what she thought was food from his tracksuit but he had told her that it must be Dean's blood. She claimed that her and a friend had been held against their will in the house until the next day when they delivered drugs to a man and they gave Lesley the money and were then set free.

Lauren McAllister, the girlfriend of Shaun Paton was the next witness. She said that she had been at Paton's home on the evening of the 3rd April and had taken heroin at his house. Lauren told the court that Paton left the house shortly after receiving a phone call from Colin Cowie and returned an hour later. According to Lauren McAllister, Paton was carrying a jacket and trainers and had blood on his own trainers. Kevin Leslie was carrying a knife and was boasting that he had just taken a boy to Elrick Hill and had stabbed him whilst fighting with him. She said that Leslie was hyper but Shaun Paton was near to tears.

We next watched a video of Shaun Paton being interviewed by the police a few days after Dean had been murdered. He wept throughout the interview. He refused to name anyone else involved and told the officers that he had received a phone call asking if he wanted to earn an easy £20.00. He claimed he got into the car with Dean who he described as fine and said that his alleged accomplices robbed him. He said that Dean had got into the car thinking it was a taxi. He said he tried to stop the others but they were laughing and said, "Let's get him to strip." Paton said he felt pure evil leaving the man out there with no clothes on. Earlier in the interview Paton wept and told officers,"I've been trying to put it to the back of my heid. I don't want anyone to get hurt, myself to get hurt for being there... I don't want slashed and stabbed and my family getting it on the outside because I spoke."

Wednesday 1st November 2006

Paton continued to be questioned and told the court that the last time he saw Dean he was upright and thought he was going to live. He said that he didn't know that they were going to take him to Elrick Hill and kill him. When told at the end of the interview that he was being arrested for the alleged murder of Dean Paton said, "I just want to say I didn't mean to do what I done. I wish I could have stopped them and myself and stopped it going further than a couple of cracks."

Tuesday 7th November 2006

Colin Cowie told the court that he was hijacked by the three accused and told to drive here, there and everywhere. He said that he didn't touch Dean and was told by the other three accused that if he talked he would be killed, his sister would be killed, that person and the next person would be killed, every man and his bloody dog would be killed, "Ye ken wit a mean."

Wednesday 8th November 2006

Christopher Gannicliffe, a police scientist, gave evidence in court that Kevin Lesley's fingerprints were found on Dean's scattered boxer shorts and his blood was found in the car's footwell. A lengthy blood trail was found along a dirt track where Dean was found wearing a long-sleeved T shirt. It was the scientist opinion that Dean had been on the ground bleeding heavily from his head wounds.

That night my friend called and asked me to meet her at the church. I was a bit bemused, she said, "The spooky church." Neither she nor myself had ever been to a spiritual church. At first I didn't want to go but for some strange reason I immediately changed my mind and agreed to meet her. There was a medium on the church stage who had come from Edinburgh and she told me that she had a message from a young man to give to me. She said that this young man had passed in tragic circumstances and that he said tomorrow will be a very harrowing day and that he would be beside me holding my hand. She also told me that I had cut off a piece of his hair as a memento. Neither this lady, nor anyone in the room, had any idea who I was.

The next day would be the evidence of the pathologist. I sat the next day in court holding an imaginary hand. I felt Dean's presence that day quite strongly. It helped me get through James Grieves' evidence.

Thursday 9th November 2006

Dr James Grieve, Pathologist, gave evidence to the court and told them that Dean had 3 stab wounds to his head; one so deep that bone was chipped from his skull. He had many other injuries on his body that was consistent with a severe beating and stabbing. He had suffered a heavy blood loss and, coupled with the severe cold, led to hypothermia. He would have been rendered confused so could not seek help or safety.

Friday 10th November 2006

Dr James Grieve continued with his evidence on the injuries that Dean sustained.

Tuesday 14th November 2006

The three remaining accused started blaming each other regarding who did what. They claimed they were afraid of any repercussions should they tell the police what happened. They contradicted everything that they had said previously. They all claimed to have tried to stop the killing.

Wednesday 15th November 2006

Kevin Lesley's turn in the witness box. He told the court that he should have done more to stop the alleged events on the night Dean died. He claimed a special defence of self defence. Lesley admitted to punching Dean with a knife but claimed to be acting in self defence. He said he had no option but to hit Dean who had ran into him whilst trying to escape. He told the court that Paton took a knife to Dean and robbed him of money and a watch, whilst Cowie riffled through his pockets.

Another witness, Professor Anthony Busuttl, told the court that if someone had turned back or got some help the injuries were not enough to kill him. Because of the head wounds and the heavy bleeding coupled with alcohol in the bloodstream would have made Dean more susceptible to hypothermia.

Thursday 16th November 2006

Teenager Malcolm Stewart told the court and jurors that he heard one of the accused "brag" about the alleged attack. He said that when the death was reported on TV Kevin Leslie boasted that he had stabbed him. Under questioning by Leslie's defence lawyer, Iain Paterson, he said that the comment in that statement was a "mistake."

Chapter 14

Friday 17th November 2006
Summing up

The jury today was due to hear closing speeches. Twelve women and three men have heard twenty-five days of evidence in the case against three men accused of murdering Dean.

Adrian Cottam, prosecutor for the crown, made his summing up statement that, "Dean was taken to Elrick Hill, stripped of most of his clothes and left there. He died cold, wet, bleeding, drunk, confused and half naked." He said that how that had, transpired and who was responsible, was up to the jury to decide.

He said Paton had told police he tried to stop the alleged incident, but did so by kicking Mr Jamieson in an effort to keep him down.

Leslie claimed he should have tried to stop what was allegedly going on, but one witness claimed he had admitted he had stabbed Mr Jamieson five times.

Another witness remembered Leslie showing her how he allegedly tried to take a "fillet" out of Mr Jamieson's side.

The twelve women and three men of the jury have also heard evidence that Colin Cowie was allegedly so worried Mr Jamieson might be dead that he had been unable to sleep that night.

Was he really another would be hero who tried to stop this? Adrian Cottam said, does the evidence tell you he was the man who could have avoided this, the one man who could have driven to Kemnay.

Mr Cottam put it to the jurors, "What do we have? Three would-be innocents in the dock? Three would-be heroes trying to stop it? Or three murderers all acting together in assaulting Mr Jamieson?"

Mr Jamieson was found dead on April 4 lying by the side of a dirt track near a golf course at Elrick Hill. It had snowed overnight and he was wearing only a long-sleeved T-shirt. He had three deep wounds, one so severe that it had chipped a bit of his skull.

Mr Cottam had alleged all three accused had acted together in a group and said in law; all those acting together in a crime are equally guilty.

He said the three accused knew when they drove away, allegedly leaving Mr Jamieson that he was so drunk he was unable to look after himself.

He said that Leslie had said the alleged victim was "in a mess" and Paton had told the police that Mr Jamieson was in such a state that the site would live with him for the rest of his life.

Mr Cottam argued that they all knew Elrick Hill was cold, dark and isolated when they assaulted and left Mr Jamieson. "They displayed such recklessness that you can be satisfied that they committed murder," he told the jury. "They simply did not care when they attacked him, they simply did not care when they left him and they showed a wicked and reckless disregard for his life."

Monday 20th November 2006

Today it is the turn of Colin Cowie's counsel to put his statement to the jury.

"Colin Cowie has admitted his guilt since day one of the trial, stressed his defence counsel Jack Davidson QC but he said appalling though the crime was, it falls short of murder." Mr Davidson was making his closing speech to the jury of twelve women and three men on the 25th day of the trial. His alleged client Colin Cowie, 22, and alleged accomplices, Kevin Leslie, also known as Mark Russell, 24, and Shaun Paton, 20, all deny murdering Dean. The trial had heard that Cowie, described as an unofficial cabbie, was allegedly flagged down by Mr Jamieson. It was claimed Leslie was a passenger in the car and that Paton was later picked up en route to Elrick Hill on the outskirts of Aberdeen where Mr Jamieson was allegedly attacked with knives, striped and robbed and left to die semi naked in the freezing cold.

He asked the jury to convict Cowie of culpable homicide, not murder. Mr Davidson reminded the jurors that on the first day of the trial, Cowie accepted his guilt to culpable homicide committed by punching Mr Jamieson repeatedly on the head and then abandoning him in freezing conditions. He asked the jury to convict Cowie of culpable homicide, and not murder.

Kevin Leslie's solicitor advocate, Iain Paterson in his closing statement said, "That none of those in the car that night had thought that Mr Jamieson was going to die." Leslie had lodged a special defence of self-defence. He said, "The leaving of Mr Jamieson up there has led to a tragedy and there is no doubt of that however, it is my submission to you that the act of leaving him up there was reckless, reckless, ill-thought and wrong." But he said, "There must be reasonable doubt in their minds about whether or not Leslie, who had apparently shown concern for Mr Jamieson after it started snowing, had the wickedness required to bring back a verdict of murder." Mr Paterson asked the jury, "Is Kevin Leslie responsible for Mr Jamieson's death? If you believe his evidence or it does not raise a reasonable doubt – yes he is. He would be guilty of culpable homicide, not murder."

Mhairi Richards QC, Paton's counsel, told the jurors that Paton had admitted his involvement right from the start, but invited the jury to return a culpable homicide conviction on her client. Lady Paton told the jurors when summing up that all three were equally guilty and had acted in unison. The jury retired to start considering its verdict.

Wednesday 22nd November2006

The Verdict

It was a nerve racking experience as we were sent out of court to wait for the verdict. We went to the little cafe at the corner of the court where we went every day for lunch. We were all nervous, not sure what the verdict would be. DS Smith had advised us to stay quiet when the verdict came in until we could leave the court and then we could rant and rave. They had hired extra police guards as the local thugs attended the court and tried to intimidate the witnesses and today there was no room left in the court to hear the verdict. After four and a half hours we were called back to court as the jury was ready to present the verdict.

The first verdict was Shaun Paton and he was convicted of culpable homicide, with a majority. A shout rang out in court and we all turned round. It was DS Smith who looked rather sheepish. I was gutted, I could not believe the verdict. He was the henchman, the one they used as the muscle. The next verdict was Colin Cowie, he was convicted of murder on a majority. Last was Kevin Leslie and he was convicted of murder in a unanimous verdict. The court room erupted and there was lots of heckling.

We the family waited until the court emptied before vacating to another room where we would discuss the verdict and then attend a Press Conference. Lady Paton deferred sentence until 22nd December.

Kevin Leslie was given 20 years, Colin Cowie 18 years and Shaun Paton 10 years for culpable homicide.

Lady Paton told Leslie, Cowie and Paton that, "It was an atrocious offence."

To assault and rob a complete stranger who was simply looking for a taxi home after a night out was evil enough. But the continued attack on Mr Jamieson amounted to a sickening and sadistic savagery, almost beyond comprehension. Everyone who heard the details felt "horror and revulsion," said the judge.

"The ultimate abandonment of Mr Jamieson in freezing conditions, at night, in remote countryside, when he was injured, bleeding and half naked, was a final and ultimately lethal act contributing to his death. His family has been left with an irreplaceable loss and a terrible grief."

An interview with Adrian Cottam was undertaken by a friend called Susan Mansfield, on the trial and how he saw it.

Susan had asked Adrian Cottam his views on the trial and he replied, "It's not one you forget." He said, "It didn't go to a jury on perversion of the course of justice that charge sits out with what they did." He informed her that his speech pulled together what our side looked at, what the evidence was, the case as he saw it, how to persuade the jury. The evidence is in the speech, the summing up.

Thereafter the Defence make a summing-up speech, they don't go into the evidence that much.

He said that Colin Cowie appealed. Kevin Leslie appealed, and then abandoned his appeal. (Possibility that Joanne withheld evidence?)

Adrian told Susan that Joanne told him to f*** off in the trial, it was on the Evening Express billboards outside. "F*** off, murder trial lawyer told." She failed to speak again. The next day, she failed to come out of the witness room; we led her evidence by way of 259, that is, got a cop to read her statement out. Her statement was compelling; her evidence was decisive in having the accused boasting about what they'd done. "I'd prefer you to shut your f***** gob," I think is what Joanne said. That's the worst I've had said to me in court.

The defence appealed on the basis that we hadn't gone far enough, we should have forced her into court, and the judge said it was fine.

The closing speech has a good summary of the evidence. It sums up the bigger points of the case, a bit about the sentence. It was described as an "unprovoked, cowardly and barbaric killing" by the judge.

Colin Stewart turned into a lead witness. He was on the periphery of it. I always had it in my mind that we would have to use him at some point to show exactly what happened. He wasn't helpful the first day he gave evidence. Almost by chance rather than design I didn't finish examining him that day, we needed to break until the following day. Overnight, he said in evidence, his dad gave him a kicking and said: 'You have to go in and tell the truth, for that boy's family'.

His version of what happened fitted with the other versions. He was a back-seat passenger. He made the case in the end. I knew the family wouldn't be very happy, with him being acquitted and called as a witness, but without him there was always a chance we wouldn't get a conviction. We had forensic evidence, but it was one word against another.

It was well put together by the police. With no witnesses, the police did well. Forensic was like the forensics you see on TV: DNA on the pants, rip in the right place. The admission of how they showed off was helpful, the witnesses didn't want to speak up. Joanne Cameron, Kevin Leslie's cousin, didn't want to, eventually accepted, and told police the truth.

It was the longest trial I've done. It was my first murder trial, and is still quite the most complex case I've done because there were four accused, and lots of strands to it. It was a case beset with silly problems.

We had all the evidence on a disk, the photographs, reports, video, then the equipment failed and we had to adjourn to get it fixed.

On the second day they thought there was a gas leak, we all had to get out of the court room.

Then Joanne and her contempt, swearing at me in court.

Then a motion to disallow some of the evidence against the first accused because a piece of paper had gone to the jury that shouldn't have.

Something different happened every day.

Susan asked Adrian what my reaction to him was and he said:

"She complained to the fiscal. Someone else dealt with the case for the first preliminary hearing. I picked it up by accident at the second preliminary hearing. It went to the then? Honorary Depute Advocate has to be allocated to someone in 5-6 weeks. The first, third and fourth accused were all represented by a QC, quite high standing. I was just there myself."

I think Jo was concerned that I was just some wee boy who wouldn't do it right and asked for someone with a wig on. The judge was complimentary (about what I did).

I remember saying to Jo, "I understand why you might say that, but I know the case, I know the area."

I was fiscal in Aberdeen for five years, I knew all the accused, knew the layout, when they were talking about this street and that, the journey to Elrick Hill. I was the only one in the whole court apart from the jury (who had that background), no other advocate depute (would have had that knowledge).

There were some points when they were speaking with quite a thick Aberdeen accent, I would say it back to them in English. The Judge said, "Is everyone happy with the advocate depute helping, because it's certainly helping me?" So that was fine.

I had prosecuted Paton lots of times for summary stuff. If you know your way around the court and that city, it does help. A QC would have come up and not known.

I had prepared a lot (of cases) as a fiscal, in charge of (cases going to) the High Court for three out of the four years, prepped but never actually prosecuted.

Susan asked Adrian, "Were you confident of a good outcome?"

Adrian said, "I'm never confident. You can have a strong case that falls on its face. And a really weak case and get a conviction. This one had so many problems which were unexpected, Joanne, the video not working, a page of the Judicial examination? Going to the jury when it shouldn't have. By the closing speech – I was confident by then. As a prosecutor, that's your bit, you're really in control of it. But I was never one hundred per cent confident. I never thought the whole thing was going to go away. But I also thought we might get Paton for murder as well."

"In my view, Paton was the ring leader, the others followed. The jury found that Leslie was the main guy, Cowie was the driver, and Paton took over and helped out a bit."

"Pathology, some photos were never shown. I drew on them quite a lot; it was important how he was lying, the state of his injuries, and his state of undress. I used a couple, before they opened him up, and Dr Grieve gave evidence (on this). There were a whole heap of photos from the internal examination which we didn't use."

Adrian said that, "You can't stop Jo seeing them if she really wants to. But Dr Grieve always says that's not him. What he is, is the person in the happy, family photos. Because (once you've seen these images) you won't forget that picture. It wouldn't have affected the jury case."

"How he was found (the position etc) was important, one of the big scenes, there is quite a lot of that in my speech."

"Police did 360-degree videos of the locus; they walked us through that (in court) with the police and Dr Grieve. Because the cause of death was primarily hypothermia and stab wounds, the internal wounds didn't make any difference; he bled to death through (more superficial wounds) as opposed to other injuries. Hypothermia and blood loss through surface wounds."

Susan asked Adrian about Colin Stewart turning Queen's evidence.

Adrian explained that he was named as one of the accused, acquitted of the charge and I called him as a witness the next day, just a normal Crown witness. The jury think he's just doing it to get off. The reason he was in (court being examined) so long, to show there was less evidence against him than the others. Build up a picture that he's not the bad guy.

The conviction came on the Tuesday. Celtic were playing Manchester United in the Champion's League, managed to get down there. We beat them, the first time ever at Parkhead.

I remember the solicitor general saying, "Fabulous result," and I said, "I can't believe Arthur saved that penalty."

I remember the front page of the Daily Record – GUILTY, and the three faces on the front, and in the corner Nakamura scoring a goal. My guilty verdict and Celtic beating Manchester United. I was delighted.

Quite ironic really as Dean was an ardent Celtic fan.

Chapter 15

Tiny Tim

Two days after the conviction of his dad's killers my little grandson Liam age nine years played the role of Tiny Tim in A Christmas Carol alongside Michael Barrymore, at his Majesty's Theatre in Aberdeen. Mr Barrymore, at the time, was fighting his own demons when a man was found floating in his swimming pool after taking a lethal cocktail of alcohol and drugs. It was claimed that due to his injuries the man, Mr Lubbock, could have been the victim of a serious sexual assault. This was a bit too close to home for Michael Barrymore and when the show ended in Aberdeen, the rest of his shows were cancelled.

Both Liam and his sister Lauren attended Stage Coach a theatre group in Aberdeen, taking after their dad who loved to perform in school plays and in general. Often you would receive a call from someone you didn't know, only to find it was Dean playing a trick on you, always the clown, he loved to make you laugh, or think he could get one up on you. On Liam's first night of performance before the curtains went up he told his mother that she would get to see him perform on stage tonight but his dad would be on stage every night to see him perform. Always the philosopher was Liam, another trait he had inherited from his dad.

As the curtain was raised my heart was in my mouth as Liam entered the stage, bursting with pride, I wept for this young lad who had so recently lost his dad. I wept for my son who was robbed of the chance to watch his son's performance, but mostly I wept for this brave young child who was not going to let the killers of his dad stand in the way of his life and as he sang his song, *The Beautiful Day*. Not a pin could be heard in the theatre, it was like time had stood still. I knew my son would be watching from above and I knew that somehow Liam was going to be alright. I sensed his future was going to be bright despite the long and arduous journey he had just been through.

The audience rose to their feet and Liam was given a standing ovation. I was beside myself both crying and clapping at the same time, I was so proud of this little boy for his courage as I knew his heart was breaking. It just goes to show how brave some children can be in the most terrible of circumstances. As I watched Liam perform I knew that Aberdeen audiences took him to their heart. He is a testament to the way that some people, even at a tender age, know they have to get on with life. His courage is in stark contrast to the cowardice of the men who killed his father. I can only hope that the killers are made aware of Liam's bravery and of the love he held for his father and how much he misses him. Perhaps then the four of them will be aware of the true cost for others of their savagery. Somehow I don't think so as sociopaths have no conscience or empathy for others.

Michael Barrymore's performance of Scrooge was a poignant reminder to the family who had watched Dean dress up as Scrooge the previous Christmas. He was a bit of a misery guts and would always moan about the cost of things, but he loved nothing more than being with family at Christmas and the previous year he had sat on a chair with a Santa hat on and pulled a grumpy face. It's one of the family's favourite reminders of Dean and has pride of place on the mantelpiece of his home. When Liam was asked if he was scared to perform in front of a lot of people he said he didn't care how many people were watching him as he would be performing for his dad. We couldn't be prouder, family travelled from Ayr to watch him perform and he was a star just like his dad.

It is amazing how kids bounce back and with the counselling in place Dean's kids were doing fine. Oh don't get me wrong, there were times when for no reason the older kids were found to be upset, but mostly they got on with life. There was an excitement in the air that no one could contain as Liam was getting ready for his performance, it was the first time since Dean had been murdered that we had something to look forward to. The rehearsals had been arduous as Liam strived for perfection and because of his age he was not allowed to perform every night. This was what the family needed: a happy event to take us up to Christmas when we knew it was going to be tough. The first Christmas without Dean. It was with a heavy heart that the preparation for Christmas began, we knew we had to make it a happy occasion for Dean's children but my heart was not in it. Christmas dinner was to be at my house and all the family including Carol and the kids would be there.

Every year since my children were young we would attend the Christmas pantomime and this year would be no different. Courtesy of the Evening Express Dean's family had the best seats in the theatre. As per usual we had dinner out before attending the theatre, I cannot remember what was playing but everyone had a good time. A couple of days to go before Christmas arrived and I was unsure whether I could pull it off, but I knew I had to for the sake of his kids. All the presents were bought and the kids were all excited. Carol didn't want to wake up on her own with the kids, so the house was extremely busy and a nightmare getting the kids to bed to enable the men to build what was needed before the children woke up.

It was rather poignant as I remembered when my kids were little and we would be trying to get the kids to bed to build the toys that needed to be built such as the bikes. The older kids went out that evening as per usual and came home a little worse for wear and it was with great hilarity that they tried to assist with the building of the toys. I was afraid that they might wake the young kids up and that would be a disaster. Eventually, I managed to calm them down and we all sat and had a nightcap as we regaled stories of all the previous

Christmases and had a laugh and a little cry as Dean would never again be around to join in and enjoy the festivities. I eventually managed to get them all to go to bed and continued to prepare Christmas lunch.

We have a tradition in the Jamieson family that everyone would have to be up before Christmas presents could be open regardless to how one was feeling after the night before and this would be no different. Santa Claus had been and there was much squealing of delight coming from the children as we all rushed downstairs including Kerrie and Gareth who were both nursing sore heads. Paul had arrived from Rugby the night before where he now lived to join in the Christmas festivities and to spend time with his two children who still lived in Aberdeen.

We all waited patiently as the children ripped open their Christmas presents. It was a joyous moment as all were focussed on the excitement of their little faces. Next it was the adults turn and finally Kerrie and Gareth excused themselves to return to the land of nod to nurse their aching heads until the next round of children arrived to open their presents and we followed the same procedure. By the time we were ready to have Christmas lunch the house was heaving. Christmas movies played in the background and there was much hilarity as both the big and the little kids were enjoying their presents.

Christmas lunch was the same every year with the usual traditional turkey and all the trimmings. Gareth and Kerrie had graced us with their presence and we toasted to absent friends and family. A hush came over the household as we remembered the previous year when we were all together as a family, including Dean and a sadness overcame us as we realised that no matter what Christmas would never be the same again. It was a really nice Christmas and after lunch we set up the Nintendo Wii and we all joined in playing games and competing against one another. There was much laughter and hilarity where everyone made the effort to ensure that the children would have a good time even though their dad would not be there.

I eventually got a seat and sat back watching them all have fun and a tear slid down my face as I thought Dean should be there playing his usual tricks and causing chaos. I breathed a sigh of relief as I realised that we had got over the first Christmas without Dean, a hurdle that I didn't think we could manage but we did and everyone had a really nice time. At last it was time to retire as I dragged myself wearily up the stairs where I could spend a few moments reflecting on the evening and crashing on to my bed I stifled a sob, unable to hold it in any longer, I fell into a fitful sleep, exhausted by the day.

Christmas over and the festivities finished, Gordon back to New Zealand and Paul back to Rugby, the house silent. Kerrie and Gareth getting on with life and I feel like I'm in limbo. I am in a kind of despair racked with guilt. I torture myself thinking I could have been a better parent. Where did I go wrong? I played the scenes of my life over and over again, and struggle to recall whatever my last conversation was before the tragedy occurred, how casual and trite it may seem now – why couldn't we have expressed our love, said a meaningful goodbye?

We judge ourselves harshly, see our faults and magnify them. Why wasn't I kinder, more generous with my time or attention?

I made lists of what I could have done but didn't do. I begged God for a moment more to love, to change to make it different or to rewrite history to take me in his place. He was young and had a life ahead of him, four children to support. Why couldn't it be me that was taken. But instead I am left with the realisation that I cannot change or alter what has happened and I have to get on with life and live with my son's murder and understand that I will never see him again. Only I don't know how. After the guilt came the anger, I would have done anything only I could do nothing. It happened and I should have been there to protect him like I did when he was young.

Dean would often sing *Angels* by Robbie Williams to me, especially when he had a drink and the words he offered me: "love and protection," would play over and over again in my head. I lived in a controlled state of rage, it would spill out when I least expected it. I remember an instance at work when I asked my Team Leader to sign a petition for prisoners who had received a life sentence and for it to mean life and she refused. I wouldn't speak to her, but on the journey home the rage consumed me and as I parked the car in my front yard I had this irresistible urge to ram the car into the front of the house.

I realised that my anger could kill me or someone else. I had to learn how to deal with it or it would destroy me. It would be sometime later before I was able to do that.

Sometimes during grief we do crazy things and I often wonder if we have lost our minds. People feel uncomfortable when you openly display your grief and they don't know what to do or say or even how to help. Society expects us to get on with life. We are told to control our feelings, the stiff upper lip and all that. So you suppress your feelings and put on the mask and act like everyone expects you to so that they feel okay in your presence and you do what is the social norm.

I realise now that feeling crazy is a normal reaction to something that has been catastrophic to you and that you are trying to handle and deal with enormously powerful feelings including the fact that your child has just been horrifically murdered and you love and miss him more than ever and just because he is dead you cannot immediately let go and pretend that all is well with the world, because it's not. It takes time to adjust to such profound and sudden absence, to be able to let go of the person's presence within your perception of your immediate world.

On December 6th, not long after the court case, I found out through the media that the three men convicted of Dean's murder were going to appeal their conviction and the length of their prison sentence. I was so consumed with rage and anger that I started drinking. I then had this crazy idea that I needed to attend Dean's grave to speak with him, so without thinking I jumped in the car and drove to the cemetery tears falling down my face, and when I arrived I found the cemetery closed. I tried to jump the gate but it was too high.

I was full of despair, I did not know what to do so I drove back home. When I arrived Gareth my son was already home and realised that I had been drinking and had drove the car. He gave me such a telling off that reality hit me like a blow to the stomach to what I had done so I phoned the police to explain to them that I had been drinking and driving and that I needed to be arrested. The police attended my house and I explained that I had been drinking and had drove to the cemetery. They spoke with Gareth and then asked for my car keys. I asked if they would be arresting me and they replied they wouldn't. Apparently, you can only be arrested if you are behind the wheel of the car.

I was so angry as I had this need to be punished as I had put myself and other lives at risk because of my recklessness. I had reached rock bottom. The next day I had to do the walk of shame and attend the police station to collect my car key and to make it worse the police were overly nice making me feel such a heel all over again. Needless to say, I have never drunk and drove ever again.

Grief leaves you with an overwhelming loss of control and I was totally out of control and was needing to get that back. Nothing would bring Dean back, but I was consumed with the injustice that victims of violence receive no support from the government whereas the criminals, the perpetrators, received every resource available such as access to psychologist, counsellors and social workers, not to take away the fact that they had a roof over their head, three meals a day and all the luxuries of a five-star hotel that provided them with computers, satellite TV and a games room. We, the victims, were struggling with accessing a counsellor for the children.

I decided that I would write to the local councillors, the Justice Minister Cathy Jamieson, the Queen and the Prime Minister regarding the inadequacies of services that must surely face those in a similar predicament. I believed that a support package should be set up as a model to guide families such as ours, ordinary, hardworking, law-abiding people, through the personal, social and economic disintegration that often accompanies the incidence of violent death.

Getting to grips with a modern justice system is never easy, and less so when it involves a trial. The notion of being able to withstand the drawn-out mechanics of a trial, and the details of a brutal attack on our flesh and blood, is one that defies comprehension. In this respect, the support for victim's family should be absolutely paramount. Instead we felt that everything was done to assuage the plight of the criminals and we were left to get on with it. Needless to say all I received were polite replies with, "Sorry for your loss," and nothing much more. It was a wasted exercise.

Chapter 16

Hope Beyond the Headlines

A violent death forces whoever survives into a nightmarish chain of events. You are surrounded by police, detectives, coroners, media, neighbours, family and the legal system. Suddenly your home is not your home - it is a makeshift interview room, a television studio and most of all a prison. You cannot escape it. You are transported into a world of chaos, shock, confusion, terror and anger overwhelms you. You are hounded by the media, intrusive questions have to be answered. Dealing with these kind of people and emotions are never easy. You have to make decisions that you never thought you would have to make such as where to bury your son.

No mother should ever have to bury their child. It is not how it is done. There is a rite of passage. The parents leave this world first, not the other way around. You find at times that you are slipping into oblivion, you cannot make sense of what has just happened. Sleep evades you and in its place nightmares takes shape, you try to cope and hold on to life but it keeps slipping away into that nightmare that is now your reality. How can you stop this chain of events, you can't you have to ride the storm, you have to find a way to stop you from being pulled into the eye of the storm. You have to find ways of coping, of surviving. You won't find it in a bottle or drugs, yes it may dull the pain for a while but you have to come up for air and when you do it thrashes into you again and again, the pain grips you like a vice right in the place where you once had a heart and the future looked bright and the sky was blue and your life was oh so perfect or at least so you thought. Now in its place hang shadows with grey skies and air that is so heavy it clogs your lungs making it practically impossible to breathe.

Finding a way how to survive the death of a loved one is different for everyone, but what I do know is that you cannot do it on your own, God knows I tried. Overcoming the death of a loved one is the most harrowing journey of all. You need to create your own support network, be it friends, relatives, or professionals, someone you can call in an emergency just to be there, make that phone call you cannot make. People often say, "Call if you need me, or can I do anything for you," take them at their word. You will need to draw strength from somewhere, people want to help. Don't shut out loved ones, they are hurting to. You may want to write a book, like me. After the event you are left with your own powerful story, putting it into words can be cathartic.

Sometimes telling the story can be painful, but keeping it in can be a burden using all your energy preventing you from getting the help that you need. The written word can be a powerful tool. The story of how your loved one died will be with you forever, you will have to tell that story over and over again and it will become bearable even though you will never forget.

You may feel anger longer and deeper than you would compared to other deaths. You need to find constructive ways to let your anger out such as a martial art, running or some form of physical exercise but at the same time give yourself lots of permission to be angry. A horrible injustice has been done to your loved one. One of the most important things that I feel is necessary is to look after yourself: have a massage, read a book, find solace away from the humdrum of everyday life. You need to take time out. Involve yourself in work or a meaningful activity but also leave time for grieving, but it's also helpful to continue with some meaningful activities and connection. The key is not to pressure yourself about accomplishments and goals.

Don't be afraid to have fun; for quite some time after the death of my son I was afraid to allow myself to be happy. I thought in some strange way he would look down and think that I had forgotten him or was no longer sad. That was not the case but give yourself permission to have fun and laugh and fill your life with as much joy as possible. Grief after murder has many expressions and everybody's grief is different and unique, like a fingerprint.

Murder is especially horrifying because another person's actions took an innocent life, as in my son's murder. This was especially difficult as the idea that the tragic loss of a loved one can be determined by another's decision, or four others in my son's case, is devastating. It can also be incomprehensible that it can be a random act. My son did not know his killers; he was in the wrong place at the wrong time. The shock of losing someone to murder takes hold immediately and leaves family members totally bewildered.

Sometimes after a loved one has died from some form of violence they may suffer from post-traumatic stress disorder (PTSD) and it can affect those who personally experience the catastrophe, those who witness it, and those who pick up the pieces afterwards including family members. It is important that you seek medical advice and get referred to a psychologist who specialises in PTSD. PTSD develops differently from person to person. While the symptoms of PTSD most commonly develop in the hours or days following the traumatic event, it can sometimes take weeks, months even years to manifest. Sometimes people are not aware they have it or they think the symptoms are normal as most people don't experience trauma in everyday life.

The traumatic event that leads to post-traumatic stress disorder is usually so overwhelming and frightening that they would upset anyone. Following a traumatic event, almost everyone experiences at least some of the symptoms of PTSD. When your sense of safety and trust are shattered, it's normal to feel crazy, disconnected or numb. It's very common to have bad dreams, feel fearful, and find it difficult to stop thinking about what happened. These are normal reactions to abnormal events. For most people, however, these symptoms are short lived. They may last for several days or even weeks, but they gradually lift. But if you have post-traumatic stress disorder, the symptoms don't decrease. You don't feel better each day. In fact, you may start to feel worse.

Bereavement groups often offer individuals an important opportunity to be with others as they allow grief to heal them. The more specific the group the better, such as a group for parents whose children have been murdered. This allows people to identify with each other and they often don't have to explain how they feel as others are going through the same process. Unfortunately for me and my family no such group existed in Aberdeen, or I didn't know about them.

Please don't be afraid to use whatever means are available to you such as counsellors, someone that specialises in bereavement. It helps to be able to speak about your loved one and to try and rationalise the intense feelings that you have and how you can address and move forward with your life in a different way as your life will never be the same. It will get easier and you owe it to your loved one to make the best life possible as you have to enjoy it mostly for your loved one as their life no longer exists in the material world.

As a family, early on we knew that we needed to get support for Dean's children, especially the oldest son Liam. He was struggling with his grief and would lash out at other children if they said anything to him. We once found him behind the sofa hitting his head on the floor and crying inconsolably. We didn't know how to help him as we were consumed with our own grief so we contacted victims support in the hope that they could point us in the right direction for an experienced child counsellor specialising in bereavement. We were informed that there was a six month waiting list. We were infuriated as Liam was in desperate need of some help and support. I used my social work contacts and found a lovely lady called Wilma that was able to assist in counselling Liam. It helped him immensely and when things got real bad for him Wilma would be at the other end of a phone or she would ensure that she had time to see him. Liam often speaks fondly about Wilma and as a family we will be eternally grateful to her as Liam has turned into a well-grounded young man and because of her expertise she has contributed to that.

Therapy offers the children the opportunity to talk about very difficult things in a safe and non-judgemental environment. The therapist or counsellor may suggest that you come with your children and that you can all talk together. Keelan, the middle child, was not too keen to speak with anyone but was happy on the odd occasion to join in. The youngest child was only three years old when his father was murdered and his way of coping was to carry a picture of his dad around with him as he was afraid that he might forget him. Tyler would have to be seen with his dad's photo at the cinema. He did that for a long time. Tyler would also be seen talking to his dad as if he was an imaginary friend. One of the times

Carol his mother said that she had been passing the living room door and she heard Tyler talking to someone telling them that they had to pay the banker money or they wouldn't get out of jail. Carol popped her head around the door and asked Tyler who was playing monopoly on his own who was he talking to and he said, "Dad silly, he won't pay his fine to get out of jail."

Carol just told him, "Then he's going to have to stay in jail then." Carol found it easier to play along with him.

I think it has been more difficult for Tyler in the long run to deal with his dad's death as he was only three years old and so has very few memories of his dad that he can remember and he can sometimes make some memories up. When he came to Australia to visit us recently we put on a DVD of when his dad was sixteen years old in Disneyland and he was really happy. He couldn't get over that his dad looked so like his brother Keelan and was a bit moody like him too. I think it is important that for children that you speak about your loved one often, as it is so easy for them to forget.

Another resource that we used was a charity called Winston's Wish that specialises in helping families cope with death. They help provide hope for children who receive timely and appropriate support. They offer information, advice and practical ideas to complement the effort of the parents, carers, teachers, professionals and other agencies supporting a child. I think that it was Faye one of our Family Liaison Officers that told us about the charity. It is based in Cheltenham,

Gloucestershire at a place called Forest of Dean - aptly named - and its mission is to provide professional services to children who have been bereaved, to enable them to live with their grief so that they can face the future with hope. Their child-focussed approach supports all the family.

After we contacted the organisation two people came to visit us to discuss the organisation and what they were able to offer us. They met all the family and discussed with Carol about whether they fitted the criteria. They spoke to the children altogether and individually about Winston's Wish and what they could expect. It sounded like fun and all agreed that they would like to attend. Tyler was too young to attend and Lauren's mother felt that she was coping well and had no need to attend. Both Liam and Keelan got a lot from attending the camp they were able to talk freely about what had happened to their dad and to know that they were not alone as there was plenty of opportunity for them to meet other children and young people from diverse backgrounds who shared similar experiences. It was invaluable for the boys to know that the feelings and fears that they were now harbouring was shared by other children who had experienced the death of a loved one through violence.

There is hope for people to move on in their lives, it doesn't mean that you can forget, it means that you live your life the best way that you can as life is precious. As you travel your journey, you will find that you are not the same person, but during that journey you need to drop the hate and the anger as it will consume you. Bring light and love with you on your journey and cherish the precious memories that you have of your loved one.

Birthdays and anniversaries will bring new challenges, especially the first year but you have to be creative. On my son's birthday I have a little ritual that I will light a candle, burn a lantern and wish him happy birthday. It is a bitter sweet day as I remember the day that he was born and I thank god that I had the pleasure to have known him and for him to have been part of my life. I have also the pleasure of his four children who either look or act the same way as Dean did so to coin a phrase of my grandson Liam who said that his dad will never die as part of him is in part of them.

Next year will be the 10th anniversary of my son's death and this year his fortieth birthday and for that day I will celebrate his life. Personally, it is the anniversary that I find the hardest and the month leading up to it. This is the day that my life was destroyed and changed forever. Regardless to how I feel, this day is the most awful, it is a constant reminder to what I lost. In the early day's I would make sure that I did something nice with the kids so that they could have nice memories, but now that I am in Australia I do my own thing. I have a massage, maybe do my nails and listen to Dean's favourite singer or a movie. I spend my time reflecting and speaking to him about his children and what we are up to now and I always light a candle. Just getting through that day is the hardest thing of all.

Chapter 17

Moving On

As I sit at the edge of Dripstone Cliffs watching the waves crash onto them, I stop to ponder. How did I get here in this hick of a town that I have grown to love, this hot, humid, sticky heat that causes the sweat to run down your back. With the sun in my face I lean back on the rocky surface oblivious to the grit getting stuck into places it shouldn't, I am transported back into time.

It was a freezing cold November day and I was shopping in Boots the chemist when suddenly my phone rang. On the other end a lady with an Australian accent uttered the words, "I believe you would like to move and work in Australia."

"I don't think so," I replied although it was tempting as it was an exceptionally cold day with temperatures below zero. "I think you have a wrong number," I advised. I thought someone was playing a prank. I had no intention of moving to the other side of the town never mind the other side of the world and leaving my surviving children and grandchildren.

Two hours later I heard myself agree to her calling me back so that I could think about it. "Where did you get my name?" I said. She told me one of my friends had given her my name. I couldn't understand it as at no time did I ever give any impression that I would like to move and work in Australia (although Australia had always been a pipe dream of mine when I was young.) My grandparents and aunties had moved to Sydney on the £10.00 assisted passage many years ago. I had never heard of Darwin with the exception of Charles Robert Darwin, the English naturalist and geologist, best known for his contribution to the evolutionary theory.

Sydney had been my dream and I had visited it a number of times in the past few years. In fact I had been on holiday to Sydney just days before Dean had been murdered. I may have moved a few years ago when my husband started working in New Zealand, but I could never have left Dean as he was too trusting and vulnerable and he needed his mother. Not that the other three children didn't. They were much more resilient. I kind of think that with your first child you are overprotective and do everything for them, leaving them less able to take care of themselves. I guess I have always had a sort of premonition that I would lose Dean early in life. Perhaps that was why I was as protective and worried about him as I was.

So I thought best to let nature take its course, I decided that if it was meant to be, so be it, and I went through the motions of having the interviews and doing the necessary paperwork for Australia. I never really put in much effort as I never really thought I would emigrate to Australia. I had to undertake a psychological assessment, that was it. I laughed, how could you assess the insane? I passed with flying colours, much to the disgust of my three children who had decided their mother was "one with flew over the cuckoo's nest." So it came as a big surprise that I was asked to move over to Darwin almost immediately.

I suddenly started feeling excited, something I hadn't felt in a long time, it started off as a quickening before it grew into the wow factor. I even started making plans for the future, something that I had given up on a long time ago after Dean had died. I had no future or so I thought, yet here was I thinking I might just do this. I had to think so I asked for a few months to consider the proposition. I asked the children what they thought and they said, "Go for it mum," secretly hoping that I would turn the offer down. Gordon, my husband, was not too keen for me to take the job as I assisted with his mother's care who was old and infirm and in a nursing home but my sister-in-law encouraged me to go saying that it was her mother and she would look after her.

Then one day as another article appeared in the newspaper about one of Dean's murderers appealing the decision to remain in prison, my mind was made up. I decided I would give it a try, my work allowed me a secondment of two and a half years so I decided I would have an adventure. I would like to think it was the universe who engineered the whole process, as up until I actually left no one thought I would, including me.

I was scared and worried, was I making the right decision, who knows. So before I knew it my husband and I were sitting at Aberdeen Airport mouths agape hardly believing that we were emigrating to the other side of the world and leaving those who were dear to us. Two years I thought and we'll be back. So it was with great trepidation that we landed at Darwin airport. I looked at Gordon and he looked at me and we giggled like two naughty schoolchildren off on an adventure.

Gordon would be flying back to work to New Zealand in a week's time and I would be starting work. I was nervous and started thinking that maybe I hadn't made the right decision after all and that I had got caught up in the moment. Palms sweating and heart racing I started to panic, I could not breathe not only was I going to be left by myself, something that hadn't happened to me ever, but I was going to be by myself alone in a strange country knowing no one. Could I do it? Was I running away? I knew my children worried about me so they felt that they should always be with me and I didn't want them to feel that way, I was being smothered, locked in a prison with no escape. I wanted them to have a life where their mother was not always worrying when they had a night out or when some article appeared in a newspaper or on the television relating to Dean causing me to spiral once again downhill back to the dark passenger. So I had a chat with myself, something I quite often use to do and decided that I would give Darwin at least two years before making my final decision, I always had a home and a job to go back to in Aberdeen and I was not a quitter.

The apartment that my work provided us with for the first few months was comfortable, near the city centre and nicely decorated. We settled quite well and for the next few days acquainted ourselves with our surroundings, checking the local amenities such as hospitals and supermarkets and it goes without saying the nearest bar. I checked out where I would be working which was in the hospital grounds.

I had not been the new kid on the block for many years and as I nervously entered the place that I would call work I had a momentary thought that I couldn't go through with it, only momentary mind you. I needn't have worried though as my colleagues were very nice and welcoming and I had nothing to fear, although it was a bit alien to me to have an office all to myself after sharing one with about thirty other social workers back home. I busied myself with attending the necessary orientation courses and through that I met many people who were soon to become my very close friends.

I would be working in the remote communities and to get there we would have to fly in planes, charter a flight, drive long distances, or by sea. I was very excited not only that, I would be working with aboriginal people. I had only ever read about them and to me they were these spiritual magical people who could tell you everything by the land and nature. The first time that I flew in a small five seated charter flight was the most magical experience I have ever had. I remember closing my eyes and hoping that Dean was with me on this fantastic journey, who would have thought that I would be travelling to work by plane dropping off at various islands and hopping back on again. I had to squeeze myself to see if it was reality, I was in heaven, the sights were magnificent. That was before I travelled in storms when the plane would drop a few feet as we hit turbulence or we swayed from side to side then fear would grip me as I begged God, angels and Dean, and whoever else that was about, to guide me safely home and my colleagues would be doubled up in laughter at my expense. This was the life, I wished I could bottle all this up for a rainy day when I would be in my old age telling my grandchildren about my great adventures. A modern day Huckleberry Finn.

There had been a batch of people from the UK who had also relocated to Darwin at a similar time; already we had something in common with each other. It was through meeting these people that Gordon and I found our first rental property right at the waterfront on the fifth floor facing out to sea. It was a glorious view to wake up to with the salty taste of the sea in your mouth and the busy activities of the boats coming in and out of the harbour or passing through. Something that you never tire of witnessing. I swear my husband knew every boat off by heart as he would sit and watch the workers hard at work. He even knew when the cruise ships were due in port as the pilot boats would anchor off to bring them in safely. You can imagine my surprise, the first time that I woke up to this massive cruise ship anchored practically on my back door. I could see the movies that they played and heard the entertainment at night when they were docked up. I had to pinch myself, was I dreaming, this was surreal. Below me at the other side of my apartment was a lagoon and a wave pool, it also consisted of a number of office blocks and restaurants, I could walk into the city centre. Everything was at my front door.

I was living the dream, every weekend a number of us would get together and take it in turns to have breakfast or lunch at each other's residence. It was like being on holiday every weekend. I was on a roller coaster and having a whale of a time, many of the people I met lived close by. We were a tight network of friends who enjoyed spending time together. Our favourite feature of the apartment would have to be the panoramic views of the most spectacular skies known to man, sunrise with its blue hue in the morning and the sunset in the evening with its array of colour from burnt orange to crimson red. It always left us speechless and in awe as we felt that that we had witnessed one of God's greatest creations until we had the greatest pleasure to witness the electrical storms as it lit up the skies with its powerful but dangerous beauty a great natural but deadly phenomena. It was with a heavy heart when we left that apartment to buy our own house until we found our dream home.

Set in an urban area was our dream home. It was by accident that we found it, my niece who was visiting had been checking all the properties online and we had been viewing some of them. Nothing had taken our fancy and we were quite despondent. We decided to just look around certain areas and came across a house that was being viewed, so we jumped out of the car to have a look. It looked good from the outside but thought it was maybe outside of our price range. We stepped inside and immediately I knew I had to have it. It had that certain wow factor, the more we looked the more excited I felt. I sensed my husband liked this one to and my niece picked her bedroom. She even told the real estate guy that it was the house for us. I laughed and thought yeah it would be real nice. I imagined myself living there, getting up in the morning and jumping into the pool for a quick dip before work. Yes, it was a nice dream. We went back to view it a few more times and we fell in love with it more and more. We decided to attend the auction and had set a price, however on the day of the auction we visited the Broker and upped our offer another $50,000.

Just before we left I had a chat with my departed loved ones and told them that I would really like the house and if they could pull any strings with him upstairs then I would really appreciate it. I jumped into the car and told my husband and niece that the house was ours. They laughed and said I was insane. However, when we arrived at the auction and saw all the people I was not so sure. Legs like jelly and nails chewed to the quick I was a nervous wreck as the bidding started. I could hardly contain myself and at one point I thought of leaving the room as I was too scared. We knew that the owners had set a price that they were willing to accept but we didn't know what it was. Suddenly it was over and we were last to bid, but it had not reached the price that the owners had wanted. I hardly dared to breathe, mouth dry I was scared to hope. The negotiations started and we eventually reached a price. I was so glad that we had upped our offer that morning of $50,000. The house was ours, who says the law of attraction doesn't work? I put it out to the universe and with a little help from our departed love ones we were now the owner of the house of our dreams. I had to pinch myself to see if it was true.

There were many things that I tried for the first time and camping was one of them, it was not something that I particularly wanted to do back home, maybe because the weather is a bit cold in Scotland, least of all sleep in a swag. I was too much of a princess and liked a bit of luxury such as a luxurious hotel room. So it was a surprise to myself when I agreed to go on a camping trip with some friends, not fully equipped, at least I had my hairdryer, hair straighteners and a pair of high heels for going out at night with. So when we reached the destination I was horrified, it was out in the middle of nowhere and there were no amenities in sight, no club and no pub. As I pulled out my hairdryer my friends all collapsed in laughter, they were seasoned campers, needless to say I have never lived it down.

I soon grew to love camping especially the roast dinners cooked on the fire in a camp oven and the fun of spending time with people who are really nice with no television or communication from the outside world as phones don't appear to work. People sat around the campfire telling stories, going for walks or swimming in the billabongs. It was so chilled out, we even went fishing, another first, if my friends could see me now back home they wouldn't believe it. Me lying under the stars at night sleeping in a swag.

Life could not be better, all my family have visited, some more than once. We visit Scotland every year, sometimes twice a year. Skype is a wonderful thing, I can speak and see my family regularly and watch the young one's grow up. I live in hope that someday they may move over to Australia to live. I'm definitely putting that out to the universe. Where once I had no future, now I'm living the dream. You can survive the loss of a child and in time it gets easier, you never forget and there is still that hole where your heart once was but you learn to live with it and I ensure that I live life to the full as it is precious and if my son hangs around I don't want him to see me miserable, I want him to be happy. Who knows what the future holds, all I know is that I am waiting for my next adventure.